U. S. Glass Co.

Decorated Satin Glass and Lamps of the 1920s

The Tiffin Glass Collectors Club

Schiffer Publishing Ltd
4880 Lower Valley Road, Atglen, PA 19310 USA

Dedication

Respectfully dedicated to the memory of Paul J. Williams, designer, mold maker, and plant engineer of the United States Glass Company, Factory R, Tiffin, Ohio.

We are indebted to his foresight in preserving the innumerable catalogs and records which provided the impetus for the publication of this volume.

Photographs by Leslie Piña.

Library of Congress Cataloging-in-Publication Data

U.S. Glass Co. : decorated satin glass and lamps of the 1920s / by the Tiffin Glass Collectors Club.
p. cm.
ISBN 0-7643-2048-3 (pbk.)
1. United States Glass Company. 2. Glassware—Pennsylvania—Pittsburgh—History—20th century. 3. Glass lampshades—Pennsylvania—Pittsburgh—History—20th century. I. Title: United States Glass Company. II. Tiffin Glass Collectors Club.

NK5198.U55U227 2004
748.2'09748'86075—dc22

2004004166

Designed by Mark David Bowyer
Type set in Americana XBd BT/Aldine721 Lt BT

ISBN: 0-7643-2048-3
Printed in China
1 2 3 4

Published by Schiffer Publishing Ltd.
4880 Lower Valley Road
Atglen, PA 19310
Phone: (610) 593-1777; Fax: (610) 593-2002
E-mail: Info@schifferbooks.com

Contents

Foreword

The Tiffin Glass Collectors Club was founded in 1985 by local collectors who were determined to keep alive an interest in the products of the Tiffin glass factory, which was being dismantled following closure the previous year. The factory, built by the A. J. Beatty and Sons Company in 1888, became Factory R of the United States Glass Company in 1892, and continued operating under that name until 1963. Although the main production consisted of blown stemware and matching tableware, many other types of ware were included in the ninety-plus years of production. The interest of the Tiffin Glass Collectors Club encompasses products from the other United States Glass factories as well.

Beginning as a small social group, the Club gradually expanded to include members from all over the United States. After bylaws were adopted, the goals of education and preservation became foremost in consideration, culminating with the opening of the Tiffin Glass Museum in November, 1998.

Following the Tiffin factory closing, and later still, the death of Paul J. Williams, former Tiffin Plant Engineer, the Tiffin Glass Collectors Club became the repository for numerous catalogs and other information from Mr. Williams' files. After examination of the paper material, it became apparent that there was information that had not been published for widespread dissemination to the general public. A decision was made to share the contents of several catalogs to aid collectors and students of depression era glassware.

Work was begun on that goal with this resulting book that focuses on a selection of table lamps and satin glass produced at Factories D, G, and K during the 1920s. Presented for the first time are color catalog pages with supplementary company advertisements, and color photos. Numerous shapes and patterns are included to emphasize the various techniques used to decorate the satin ware. Readers should be aware that, due to the size of the United States Glass Company and the immense volume of items produced, these articles represent only a small percentage of the total output of Factories D, G, and K.

The dimensions are measured at the widest point, with an "h" indicating the height as the largest dimension of the object. Company terminology is used in the captions to describe items, with object and color names capitalized. Line numbers usually consisted of a five-digit number, i.e. #15310; however, some catalog pages reference only the final three digits, i.e. #310.

The following criteria was used for color definition: (1) Color names were obtained from United States Glass Company catalog pages. (2) Descriptive terms from company advertisements were used to define color hues when the catalog pages were unobtainable. (3) Color names that have been adopted and accepted by collectors for recognition purposes have been used when company documentation was lacking, and these are in lower case.

Prices are listed in U. S. dollars in the captions. These values are retail prices for items in perfect condition, derived from actual purchase prices, from prices seen at antique shows or shops, and Internet auctions. Rarity and desirability were taken into consideration as well. The values are intended as a guide, and neither the Tiffin Glass Collectors Club nor the publisher is responsible for any transaction based on this guide.

We are indebted to the following friends for providing glassware and information to give readers a more useful resource and to add to the enjoyment of this volume: Howard and Janet Beisner, Melissa Bratkovich, Neila and Tom Bredehoft, Stan and Joyce Brown, Carol J. Chaney, Brian Courtney, Eunice Cover, The Gallery-Richard and Beverly Digby, Dick and Ginny Distel, Phil and Rayella Engle, Russ Gangloff, Brett Goshe, Ed Goshe, Lyman and Ruth Hemminger, Madolyn Nichols Key, Ruth Ann Leonard, Carolyn Menta, Kelly O'Kane, Robert and Donna Overholt, Bill Reyer, Nancy Rubenstein, Angela Van Riper, Tiffin Glass Collectors Club, Tiffin Glass Museum, and the family of Paul J. Williams. Special gratitude is given to Leslie Piña for her photography of the color photos and the donation of her labor. We are also grateful to our editors, Donna Baker, Douglas Congdon-Martin, and Ginny Parfitt for their assistance and expertise in preparing this book.

History of the United States Glass Company

The United States Glass Company came into operation on July 1, 1891, as a conglomerate composed of fifteen glass companies, with headquarters located at Ninth and Bingham Streets in Pittsburgh, Pennsylvania. The reason for the merging of the factories was to reduce costs by eliminating competition with one another and to control production levels. After joining U. S. Glass, the companies lost their national identities, and the parent company identified them by a letter. The fifteen glass companies that joined in 1891 were: Adams and Company; Bryce Brothers; Challinor, Taylor, and Company; George Duncan and Sons; Richards and Hartley; Ripley and Company; Gillinder and Sons; Hobbs Glass Company; Columbia Glass Company; King Glass Company; O'Hara Glass Company; Bellaire Goblet Company; Nickel Plate Glass Company; Central Glass Company; and Doyle and Company.

Many of the original factories failed due to fires or natural gas shortages. A plan was developed by management to consolidate the remaining factories in one area; however, as revealed in a February 27, 1924, stockholders' report, the plan was never implemented. This report reads in part:

> The question has been asked at different times, as to why the plants were not consolidated under one roof, and one factory manager. Shortly after the consolidation of the factories, composing the United States Glass Company at that time, it was proposed to eventually locate all the plants at one place and five hundred acres of land were bought a few miles above the city of McKeesport on the Monongahela River about twenty miles from Pittsburgh, afterwards known as Glassport. Later on for legal reasons, it was separated from the Glass Companies assets and became the Glassport Land Company, the entire Capital Stock of which was, and still is, owned by your company.
>
> A factory was built upon the property but it soon became evident that it was not feasible, nor possible, to dismantle and remove the Pittsburgh factories to Glassport without tremendous expense and the loss of much of the necessary skilled, as well as other labor.
>
> At about this same period the Company was offered a plot of ground at Gas City, Indiana, with practically free natural gas; to take advantage of that, and with the idea of having a factory whose freight rates to the west would be advantageous, a large plant was built: for a time the advantage was great; but unfortunately, no reserve was set up for the time when natural gas would cease to exist in that territory and in due course of time, off and on, the plant became a burden, as did also the plant at Glassport both of which, however, I believe have passed through their troubles and are now in position to steadily go forward.
>
> If it were feasible to have all the plants under one roof, it would be utterly impractical to make the varied lines under one factory management. The very nature of your business requires personal initiative in the way of making designs and shapes, with ever-changing styles and peculiar methods of manufacture, which no one person could possibly encompass. A visitor to your showroom on Liberty Avenue, this city, will clearly demonstrate this point.
>
> One great advantage in not having the plants consolidated is the fire risk. At present should one factory be destroyed at least portions of the business could be transferred to other factories – also freedom from petty labor troubles that do not affect all plants when they occur at one factory.

Identification of some of the factories is difficult, because the letter designations given to the original factories were later given to other factories. The following is a list of factories and letter designations of the U. S. Glass companies. Members of the original combine in 1891 will be designated by an * after the factory letter.

*Factory A** – Adams and Company was located at South Tenth and Winnebago Streets in Pittsburgh, Pennsylvania. The factory was known for pattern glass lines, soda fountain items, jugs, and fish globes. It continued with U. S. Glass through the mid 1940s.

*Factory B** – Bryce Brothers was located in Pittsburgh, Pennsylvania, at South 21st and Wharton Streets. It produced many pattern glass lines as well as birdbaths, seed cups, candy trays and jars, and lamps. Production ended in 1931.

*Factory C** – Challinor, Taylor, and Company was located at Tarentum, Pennsylvania. Products included pattern glass lines, lampshades, and opal ware. The factory was destroyed by fire shortly after joining the combine and was not rebuilt.

Factory C – In 1910, company records listed a Factory C as a decorating department, occupying one and a half floors at Factory E, Tenth Street, Pittsburgh, Pennsylvania.

Factory D⋆ – George Duncan and Sons was a member of the original combine. Fire destroyed the factory in 1892. The principal shareholders left the company and formed the Duncan and Miller Glass Company in Washington, Pennsylvania.

Factory D – In 1904, U. S. Glass founded a factory at South Tenth Street in Pittsburgh, Pennsylvania which was used exclusively for decorating. Gold, silver, and painted ware was produced at this location until 1931.

Factory E⋆ – Richards and Hartley was located at Tarentum, Pennsylvania. Records are unclear when their association with the combine ended.

Factory E – Located at South Tenth and Sarah Streets, Pittsburgh, Pennsylvania. Factory E was operating as early as 1902, producing pressed tumblers and table glassware. Interestingly, a bridge connected Factories A and E. Operations ceased in 1931.

Factory F⋆ – Ripley and Company was located at Eighth, Ninth, Bingham Streets, and Cabot Way in Pittsburgh, Pennsylvania. Primary products included pressed tableware and confections jars. The U. S. Glass headquarters was located here until 1937; however, factory operations ceased in 1931.

Factory G⋆ – Gillinder and Sons, Greensburg, Pennsylvania, were manufacturers of pressed ware and novelty items. Records do not indicate any production in 1894. The 1907 stockholders report stated the Greensburg factory was sold the previous fiscal year for $60,000.

Factory G – In 1894, U. S. Glass built and operated a new factory located at Seventh Street, Glassport, Pennsylvania. Operations included the manufacture of pressed ware, including satin glass during the 1920s and 1930s era. Following the company's reorganization in 1937, only factories A, G, and R remained, with the latter two factories the primary manufacturers. Factory G was destroyed by a tornado on August 3, 1963.

Factory GCS, (Glassport Cutting Shop) and Factory GED, (Glassport Etching Department) were in operation in the late 1920s at Glassport, Pennsylvania.

Factory H⋆ – Hobbs Glass Company, located at Wheeling, West Virginia, produced pressed tableware. The factory ceased to be a part of U. S. Glass c. 1893-1894.

Factory H – In 1910, company records indicate that a Factory H was a decorating shop located at Southside, Pittsburgh, Pennsylvania.

Factory H – 1925 U. S. Glass records listed a Factory H at Glassport, Pennsylvania.

Factory J⋆ – Columbia Glass Company was located along the east side of the New York Central Railroad, between Crystal Avenue and the Nickel Plate Railroad in Findlay, Ohio. Production consisted of pressed tableware lines. Closure occurred in December 1892, as a result of a citywide natural gas shortage.

Factory K⋆ – King Glass Company was located at South Eighteenth and Merriman Streets in Pittsburgh, Pennsylvania. This factory produced satin glass and decorative ware. Operations ceased in 1931.

Factory L⋆ – O'Hara Glass Company, located in Pittsburgh, Pennsylvania, was an original company member, but ceased operations on June 30, 1893.

Factory L – Records from 1919 and 1923 indicate another Factory L was located at South 21st and Wharton Streets in Pittsburgh, Pennsylvania. Production was limited to lighting globes. Operations were discontinued in 1925.

Factory M⋆ – Bellaire Goblet Company was located along the west side of Bolton Street between College and Davis Streets in Findlay, Ohio, and manufactured tableware. Production ended in December, 1892, as a result of a natural gas shortage.

Factory M – Reference is made in 1929 to a Factory M at Seventh Street, Glassport, Pennsylvania. The factory specialized in machine-made bowls and jars as late as 1935.

Factory N⋆ – Nickel Plate Glass Company was located adjacent to the Nickel Plate Railroad tracks and within the Nickel Plate subdivision of Fostoria, Ohio. This factory was known for its opalescent lamps and tableware. Operations ceased August, 1893, and the plant was destroyed by fire August 28, 1895.

Factory N – In 1910, U. S. Glass built a decorating facility located at Seventh Street, Glassport, Pennsylvania, and identified it as Factory N. Records indicate this factory was still in operation in 1935.

Factory O⋆ – Central Glass Company was located in Wheeling, West Virginia. A producer of pressed tableware, the factory was closed in October, 1893, and was sold in 1895.

Factory O – A new manufacturing plant was built in 1910, by U. S. Glass at Seventh Street, Glassport, Pennsylvania, and was named Factory O. This factory produced confection jars and blown and pressed ware. Records indicate production continued through at least 1935.

Factory P⋆ – Doyle and Company was located in Pittsburgh, Pennsylvania. This cutting shop was still in operation in 1895. Date of closure is unknown.

Factory R – A. J. Beatty and Sons Company was purchased by U. S. Glass January 1, 1892, and named Factory R. Located in the Highland addition, Tiffin, Ohio, it was bordered by Fourth, Sneath, and Shawhan Avenues. The factory produced pressed tumblers, and later became known for its blown stemware and tableware. The corporation reorganized in 1937, and the U. S. Glass headquarters was moved to Tiffin, Ohio, the following year. Bankruptcy occurred in 1962. The Tiffin factory was sold to Tiffin Art Glass in 1963, signaling the end of the United States Glass Company.

Factory S – Reference is made to Factory S as a warehouse facility of the A. J. Beatty and Sons factory in Steubenville, Ohio. In 1892, the warehouse was purchased with the assets of the A. J. Beatty and Sons plant in Tiffin.

Factory S – A decorating department at Factory R in Tiffin, Ohio, was designated as Factory S in company records from the 1920s and 1930s.

Factory T – Novelty Glass Company, located at Buckley and Sandusky Streets in Fostoria, Ohio, was purchased by U. S. Glass on October 6, 1892. Factory T produced blown tumblers and stemware. The factory was partially destroyed by fire on April 1, 1893, and production ceased at that time. Sale of the property took place in February, 1896.

Factory U – U. S. Glass began the construction of Factory U at Gas City, Indiana, in September, 1893. Primary production consisted of pressed tableware. U. S. Glass operated the factory until 1935.

Factory X – A 1925 record referred to a Factory X located at Gas City, Indiana.

The Pittsburgh Stock Exchange Security Committee Bulletin dated March 20, 1923, contains a list of the factories at that time. It reads in part:

> On January 27, 1923 the Board of Directors offered to its stockholders for subscription 40,000 new shares of the Capital Stock of the Company, which was necessary to complete the refinancing of the Company.
>
> BUSINESS – The Company manufactures chiefly pressed and blown table glassware but does not completely confine itself to the production of these articles. It manufactures any product that can be made with similar equipment such as confectioner and druggist display jars, tobacco jars, hotel, restaurant and soda fountain supplies, lamps, battery jars, electrical and instrument covers, etc. It is estimated, that including the different etchings and cuttings, as well as shapes and designs, the factories make over 30,000 different articles. The Company has fifteen sales offices, eleven domestic and four foreign – located in the following cities: Pittsburgh, Pa., New York, N. Y., Boston, Mass., Philadelphia, Pa., Baltimore, Md., Chicago, Ill., Denver, Colo., San Francisco, Cal., Los Angeles, Cal., St. Louis, Mo., Dallas, Tex., London, England, Sydney, Australia, Mexico City, Mexico and Havana, Cuba.
>
> PLANT AND EQUIPMENT – The company, at the present time, comprises nine manufacturing plants – five in Pittsburgh, Pa., two in Glassport, Pa., one in Tiffin, Ohio and one in Gas City, Indiana; two general decorating shops and one special shop. A detailed description of the factories is given as follows:
>
> FACTORY A – Located on the Southside, Pittsburgh. Occupies nearly an entire square, bounded by Winnebago, Tenth, Selby Alley and Ninth Streets. Consists of two-story brick factory buildings, equipped with modern sprinkler system. It operates a 20-ton continuous tank with muffled lehrs; modern Chapman Gas Producers for making gas from coal and also, an oil burning system and facilities for burning natural gas; a mould and machine shop with complete lines of moulds, tools and general equipment for the manufacture of a general line of table glasses, pressed and blown specialties as battery jars, headlight lens, etc. The plant has been remodeled within the past four years by installing an entire new furnace, lehrs and producer systems.
>
> FACTORY B – Located on the Southside, Pittsburgh. Occupies an entire square, bounded by Twentieth, Wharton, Twenty-First Streets and Fox Alley and a large part of a square bounded by the same streets and Merriman Alley. The main factory occupies adequate two-story brick buildings, while the packing rooms, office, warehouses and shipping rooms are housed in a one and two-story brick and partly frame buildings, all equipped with a modern sprinkler system and adjacent to direct railroad sidings. It is equipped with a modern 18-ton regenerative type continuous tank; a 12 pot Deepeye type furnace; modern Chapman type gas producers for making gas from coal; and also equipped to burn fuel oil as well as natural gas, complete mould and machine shop, with full lines of moulds and tools. It manufactures special lines of pressed and blown glassware such as lighting glassware, lamps, jars, etc.
>
> FACTORY D – Located on the Southside, Pittsburgh. Occupies nearly an entire square bounded by Sarah, Tenth, and Eleventh Streets. This plant is exclusively a decorating plant. It is equipped with modern sprinkler system; modern decorating lehrs, kilns, etc. and all facilities for decorating all types of tableware, lighting glass, lamps, etc. It also has adequate shipping and warehouse facilities.
>
> FACTORY E –Located on the Southside, Pittsburgh. Occupies the entire square bounded by Ninth, Tenth, Sarah Streets and Selby Alley. Consists of a three-story brick building, brick factory buildings and a frame warehouse. The plant is equipped with modern sprinkler system; a 20-ton regenerative type continuous tank; Chapman type gas producers for making gas from coal; storage tanks for burning fuel oil as well as gas; adequate lehrs; complete mould and machine shop with full lines of moulds. The plant is exclusively an automatic machine factory and has been recently remodeled. It operates Miller type Automatic Feeders and Presses and makes a general line of pressed tumblers and table glassware.
>
> FACTORY F – Located on the Southside, Pittsburgh. Occupies an entire square bounded by Eighth, Ninth, Bingham Streets and Cabot Way. It consists of substantial two and three-story brick buildings. The General Offices of the Company are located in connection with this factory. The factory is equipped with two Deepeye furnaces with a total capacity of 25 pots;

storage tanks for burning oil as well as natural gas and a modern sprinkler system. It manufactures special lines of pressed and blown glassware as electrical instrument covers, door knobs and display jars. Included with this plant is a two-story brick warehouse located on Carson Street between Eighth and Ninth Streets.

FACTORY G – Located at Glassport, Pa. Occupies approximately 3.6 acres of ground with substantial two-story brick factory buildings, a large brick warehouse and a two-story brick cooperage plant. This plant has its own railroad siding. It is equipped with two modern 15 pot regenerative type furnaces with Chapman type producer plant for making gas from coal, as well as a complete system for burning fuel oil, which are of the latest type, having been installed within the last four years; adequate storage tanks etc., as well as facilities for burning natural gas; a modern sprinkler system; adequate lehrs; a mould and machine shop with a complete line of moulds, tools and all the necessary equipment for the manufacture of exclusive lines of pressed table glassware for both export and domestic trade.

FACTORY K – Located on the Southside, Pittsburgh, on Eighteenth and Merriman Streets. It consists of two and three-story factory buildings, a brick office building and a three-story warehouse. It is equipped with storage tanks, etc. for burning fuel oil, as well as facilities for burning natural gas; a modern sprinkler system; two Deepeye type furnaces with a total capacity of 25 pots and three, 1 and 2-ton day tanks; adequate lehrs; large mould and machine shop with complete lines of moulds, tools and equipment; a cutting shop with a capacity of about 50 frames; a modern etching shop. The plant manufactures complete lines of pressed table and decorative glassware, in both crystal and colors, and specialties such as knobs, etc. It also has excellent railroad facilities.

FACTORY O – Located at Glassport, Pa. Occupies about 3.5 acres with railroad siding. It consists of two and three-story brick factory buildings. It is equipped with modern sprinkler system; one 40-ton regenerative type continuous tank with Chapman type producer system for making gas from coal, as well as a system for burning fuel oil and natural gas; ample lehrs; complete mould and machine shop with full lines of moulds, tools and equipment; a decorating shop with lehr for firing ware and a decorative cutting shop with a capacity of about thirty frames. The plant manufactures a general line of pressed table glassware, special lines of pressed and blown ware, such as tobacco jars, confection jars, etc., and a general line of blown tumblers and stemware.

FACTORY R – Located at Tiffin, Ohio. Occupies about 6.4 acres of land. The factory proper occupies modern two-story brick buildings. There is also a two-story brick cutting shop with a capacity of approximately 140 frames; modern two-story etching and decorating shops; large iron clad warehouses and frame office buildings. It is equipped with a modern sprinkler system; two modern 18 pot regenerative type furnaces; a modern automatic Woods producer for making gas from coal; adequate coal storage, conveyers, crusher and all facilities for handling and storing coal; a complete system for burning fuel oil with storage tanks etc., as well as facilities for burning natural gas; lehrs; a mould and machine shop with complete equipment of moulds, tools, etc. The plant manufactures complete lines of lead blown glassware, stemware, tumblers, tableware of all descriptions, with modern facilities for producing decorations; cut, etched and decorated wares. The entire furnaces and fuel systems are new, having been installed within the last four years. It also has excellent railroad siding facilities.

FACTORY U – Located at Gas City, Indiana. Situated on about 21 acres of land. It consists of a two-story brick building with steel iron clad factory building; large iron clad warehouse; mixing and material storage building; Cooper shop and a modern brick office building. The plant has its own railroad siding. It is equipped with modern sprinkler system; two regenerative type continuous tanks, each with an approximate capacity of 20-tons per day; one regenerative type 16 pot furnace; Chapman type producer gas plant for making fuel gas from coal and a complete system for burning fuel oil, storage tanks etc. and also facilities for burning natural gas; adequate lehrs; a large mould and machine shop, with full lines of moulds and tools; a cutting shop with a capacity of 12 frames. One of the tanks at this plant is built and equipped with Miller Automatic Feeders and Presses for making automatic machine ware exclusively. It manufactures a general line of pressed and blown glassware and specialties, in both crystal and colors.

OFFICERS: Marion G. Bryce, President; David Yost, Vice President; Ernst Nickel, Secretary-Treasurer; Harvey Wilson, Assistant Treasurer; Wm. R. Nickel, Assistant Secretary.

DIRECTORS: L. Z. Birmingham, Marion G. Bryce, Jas. F. Challinor, Rueben Haley, L. A. Meyran, Ernst Nickel, H. N. Trimble, C. E. Willock, David Yost, all of Pittsburgh, Pa.

China, Glass and Lamps advertisement, April 11, 1927. The gold-colored label was used on company products prior to 1927. It was comprised of the intertwined letters, "U, S, G, and Co."

Beginning September, 1927, the Tiffin paper label was used on United States Glass products. The word "Tiffin" is printed over a large "T" within a shield.

The Tiffin label with the wording "Hand Made Tiffin" came into usage c. 1950. This label was never used on satin glass products.

Green and Blue, 6" h. U. S. Glass logos with a satin finish. The logos have the intertwined U. S. Glass Co. insignia within the shield, with the word "Quality" below it. Around the base are the words, "United States Glass," in block lettering. Black 6" h. Tiffin logo with gold encrustation. The logo has an upper case "T" in the shield with the word, "Tiffin," through the "T." The base has "United States Glass" in block lettering around it. The Tiffin Glass Collectors Club currently owns the mold for the Tiffin logo. They have reproduced the logos in the colors of pink, ruby, cobalt blue, green, purple, and yellow. Some logos have a satin or iridized finish.

A decision was made in September, 1927, to market all United States Glass decorative wares as Tiffin or Tiffinware, regardless of factory origin. This was a marketing ploy to take advantage of the reputation of the fine quality glassware produced at the Tiffin, Ohio, factory. A gold paper label with the word "Tiffin" was used in place of the U. S. Glass label. This practice continued until the demise of the United States Glass Company in 1963. Glass prototypes of the U. S. Glass and Tiffin shield marks were distributed to dealers of U. S. Glass products for display purposes.

Financial difficulties plagued the company in the middle 1930s. In June, 1938, the U. S. Glass headquarters was moved to Tiffin, Ohio. At this time only three glass factories remained. The Glassport factory was designated to produce crystal and opal pressed ware, and the Tiffin factory's focus was on blown ware in crystal and colors. The Adams factory in Pittsburgh remained in operation through the mid 1940s, producing opal liners for zinc lids.

The 1940s were prosperous due to the introduction of new colors and the Swedish Modern line at the Tiffin factory. The purchase of molds from the defunct Duncan and Miller Glass Company in 1955 brought additional sales. After two decades of success, financial difficulties arose due to an influx of inexpensive imports and higher operating costs, resulting in the sale of the company assets in 1958 to a New York investment firm. In March, 1961, a second sale took place to Brilhart Plastics Corporation of Mineola, New York. Bankruptcy occurred in 1962; however, the Tiffin factory remained open until early 1963. Four former Tiffin Glass employees purchased the Tiffin factory in 1963 and named it the Tiffin Art Glass Corporation. On August 3, 1963, the Glassport factory was destroyed by a tornado. These events marked the conclusion of the United States Glass Company, a manufacturing giant that left an indelible record in the history of glassmaking.

China, Glass and Lamps advertisement, April 13, 1925.

Color Guide

The complex process of glassmaking often results in a wide variation of colors with the finished product exhibiting many different shades under varying circumstances. Degrees of brightness or more subdued hues may appear in different batches. Quality control of raw materials and numerous other factors can determine the final color. Glass collectors readily accept these variances and enjoy them as a part of the nature of the glassmaking process.

This color guide includes the major colors utilized by the U.S. Glass Company at the time of production of the items selected for this publication. Several color variations were used for special treatment purposes; however, these were in use for a limited time and for the production of specific items. Examples are the colors of the Carrara and the stretch glass products.

Amethyst. A medium purple, also marketed as Royal Purple or Mulberry, with limited production.

Amber. A dark honey color with brown overtones. Extensive stemware production.

Black. A translucent black. Extensive production in satin finish.

Blue (Sky Blue). A light blue color.

Crystal. Crystal refers to colorless glass. The company name for crystal with a satin finish was white satin.

Canary. A bright yellow that fluoresces yellow-green when placed under ultraviolet lighting. Many collectors often refer to this color as vaseline.

Green (Emerald Green). A true medium green.

Lilac. A pale lavender color introduced in 1926. Primarily produced at Factory R.

Green (Reflex Green). A light pastel green which fluoresces yellow-green under ultraviolet light.

Old Gold. An amber-toned yellow which fluoresces tangerine under ultraviolet light. Introduced in 1928.

Jasper. A dark blue-green color. Limited production.

Pink (Rose Pink). A pale pink, sometimes with an orange cast.

Royal Blue. A true deep cobalt color.

Red. A red, shading to areas of orange and yellow, introduced in 1923. Collectors often refer to it as amberina.

Ruby. A true deep red. Limited production.

Twilite. A blue with lavender tones, introduced in 1928.

Chapter 1

Painted Decorations

Morning Glory. 1928 catalog page, Factory D.
Top Row: $75, $65, $65, $65.
Middle Row: $75, $55 pair, $65, $45.
Bottom Row: $75, $45, $45, $55 set.
Also note the Tiffin shield on the catalog page. In September, 1927, U. S. Glass started to market all their decorative wares as Tiffin, regardless of which factory manufactured the item. This practice continued through the company's closure in 1963. The Tiffin gold label is occasionally found on satin ware from the 1920s and 1930s.

Morning Glory.
Pink Satin:
#8105, 10" Rolled Edge Salad Bowl. $65.
#15151, 8" h. Cupped Dahlia Vase. $75.
The decoration is a cluster of morning glory flowers in red, blue, orange, and yellow with gold scrollwork. Also found on green satin blanks.

Morning Glory.
Green Satin:
#93, 5" Low Candleholders. $55 pair.
#179, 10" Handled Cake Plate. $55.
Pink Satin #319, 13" Rolled Edge Table Center. $75.

Detail of **Morning Glory** decoration.

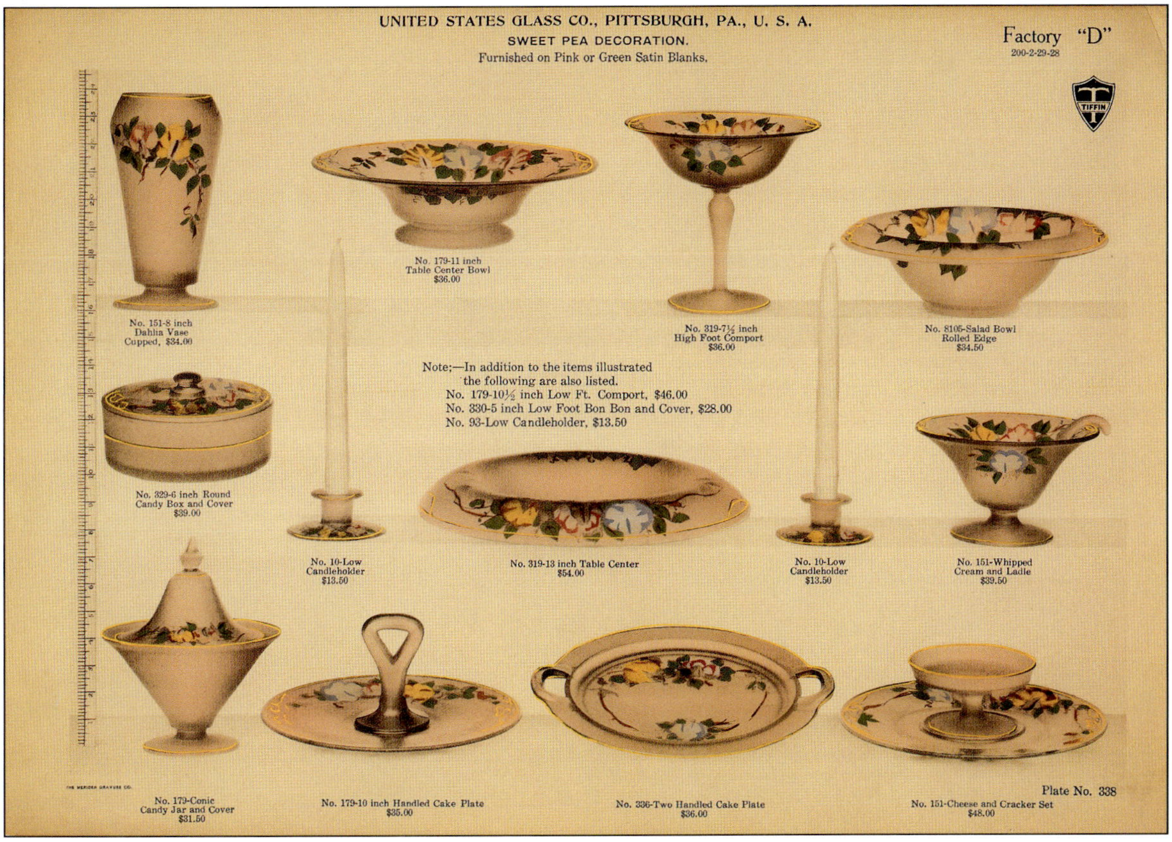
UNITED STATES GLASS CO., PITTSBURGH, PA., U. S. A.
SWEET PEA DECORATION.
Furnished on Pink or Green Satin Blanks.

Factory "D"
200-2-29-28

No. 151-8 inch Dahlia Vase Cupped, $34.00

No. 179-11 inch Table Center Bowl $36.00

No. 319-7½ inch High Foot Comport $36.00

No. 8105-Salad Bowl Rolled Edge $34.50

Note;—In addition to the items illustrated the following are also listed.
No. 179-10½ inch Low Ft. Comport, $46.00
No. 330-5 inch Low Foot Bon Bon and Cover, $28.00
No. 93-Low Candleholder, $13.50

No. 329-6 inch Round Candy Box and Cover $39.00

No. 10-Low Candleholder $13.50

No. 319-13 inch Table Center $54.00

No. 10-Low Candleholder $13.50

No. 151-Whipped Cream and Ladle $39.50

No. 179-Conic Candy Jar and Cover $31.50

No. 179-10 inch Handled Cake Plate $35.00

No. 336-Two Handled Cake Plate $36.00

No. 151-Cheese and Cracker Set $48.00

Plate No. 338

Sweet Pea. 1928 catalog page, Factory D.
Top Row: $75, $65, $65, $65.
Middle Row: $75, $55 pair, $65, $45.
Bottom Row: $75, $45, $45, $55 set.

Detail of **Sweet Pea** decoration.

Sweet Pea.
Pink Satin:
#336, 11.25" Two Handled Cake Plate. $45.
#15151, 8" h. Cupped Dahlia Vase. $75.
The Sweet Pea decoration is a hand-painted design with gold scrollwork, found on pink and green satin blanks. Decorated at Factory D.

Helio.
Pink Satin:
#15151, 8" h. Cupped Dahlia Vase. $75.
#15319, 12" Rolled Edge Fruit Bowl. $65.
Found on pink satin blanks, Helio is a hand-painted decoration of heliotrope flowers with gold scrollwork.

Detail of **Helio** decoration.

UNITED STATES GLASS CO., PITTSBURGH, PA., U. S. A.
AUTUMN LEAF DECORATION
Furnished on Pink Satin Blanks only.

Factory "D"
200-2-29-23

No. 151-8 inch Dahlia Vase Cupped, $34.00

No. 179-11 inch Table Center Bowl $36.00

No. 319-7½ inch High Foot Comport $36.00

No. 8105-Salad Bowl Rolled Edge $34.50

Note;—In addition to the items illustrated the following are also listed.
No. 330-10 inch Low Foot Comport, R/E. $39.00
No. 93-Low Candleholder, $13.50

No. 329-6 inch Round Candy Box and Cover $39.00

No. 10-Low Candleholder $13.50

No. 319-13 inch Table Center $54.00

No. 10-Low Candleholder $13.50

No. 151-Whipped Cream and Ladle $39.50

No. 179-Conic Candy Jar and Cover $31.50

No. 179-10 inch Handled Cake Plate $35.00

No. 336-Two Handled Cake Plate $36.00

No. 151-Cheese and Cracker Set $48.00

Plate 335

Autumn Leaf. 1928 catalog page, Factory D. Top Row: $75, $65, $65, $65. Middle Row: $75, $55 pair, $65, $45. Bottom Row: $75, $45, $45, $55 set.

Autumn Leaf.
Pink Satin:
#329, 6" Round Candy Box and Cover. $75.
#15179, 9" Low Foot Flared Comport. $65.
#179, 7.5" h. Conic Candy Jar and Cover. $75.
Decorated at Factory D, the design consists of leaves painted in autumnal colors with gold scrollwork. There is also an inventory listing for the #319 table center bowl and #10 low candleholders in green satin.

Detail of **Autumn Leaf** decoration.

Detail of **Roses** decoration

Roses.
Pink Satin #179, 7.5" h. Conic Candy Jar. $75.
The Roses decoration is found on pink satin blanks. The design consists of hand-painted roses with gold scrollwork. Decorated at Factory D.

Pink Satin #103, 12" h. Cylinder Vase, **Palm** decoration. $125.
Blown and decorated at Factory R.

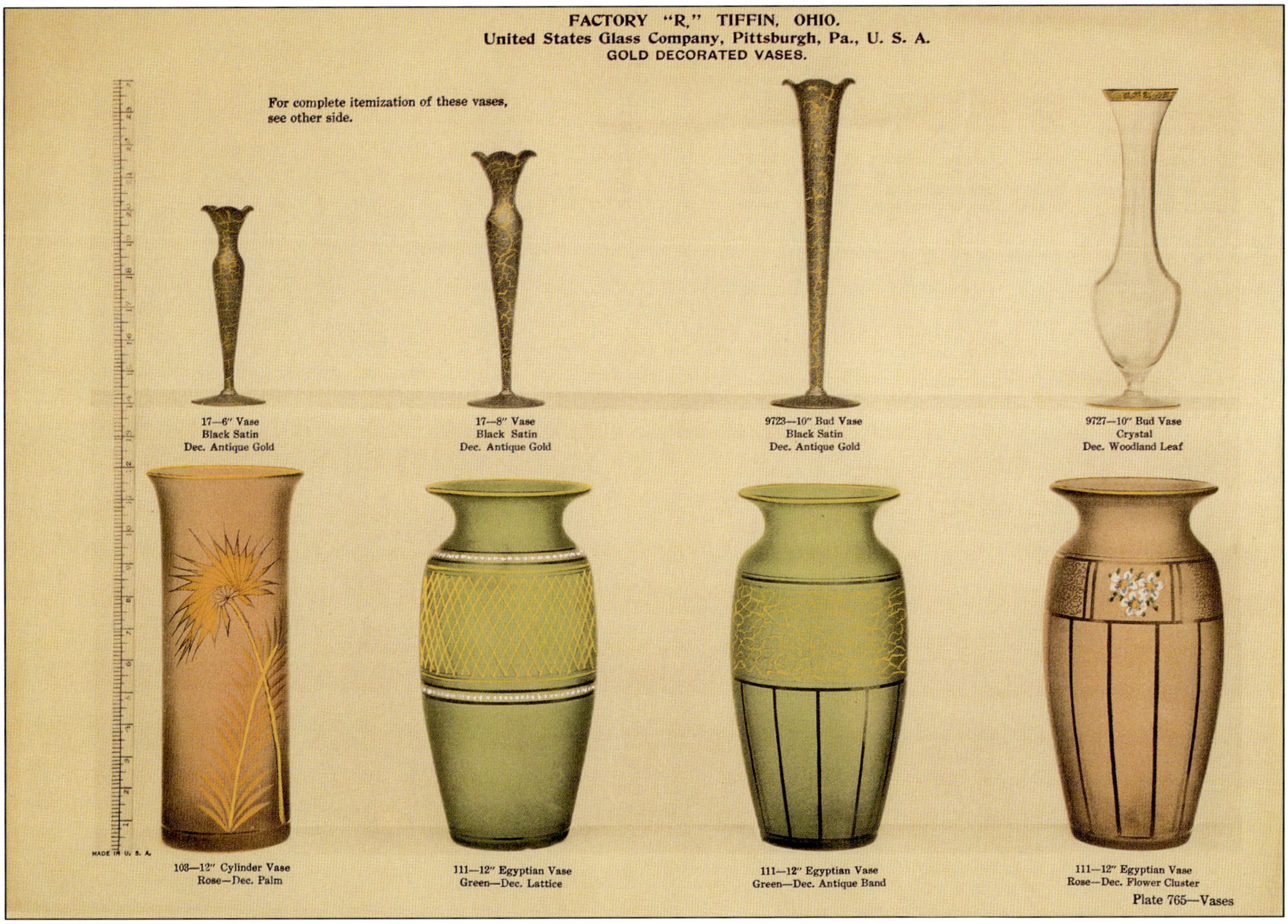

Gold Decorated Vases. Undated catalog page, Factory R.
Top Row: $35, $45, $55, $25.
Bottom Row: $125, $135, $135, $135.

Alaska. 1927 catalog page, Factory GED.
Top Row: $50, $65, $50.
Middle Row: $65, $55 pair, $50, $65 set.
Bottom Row: $45, $55, $55 set.

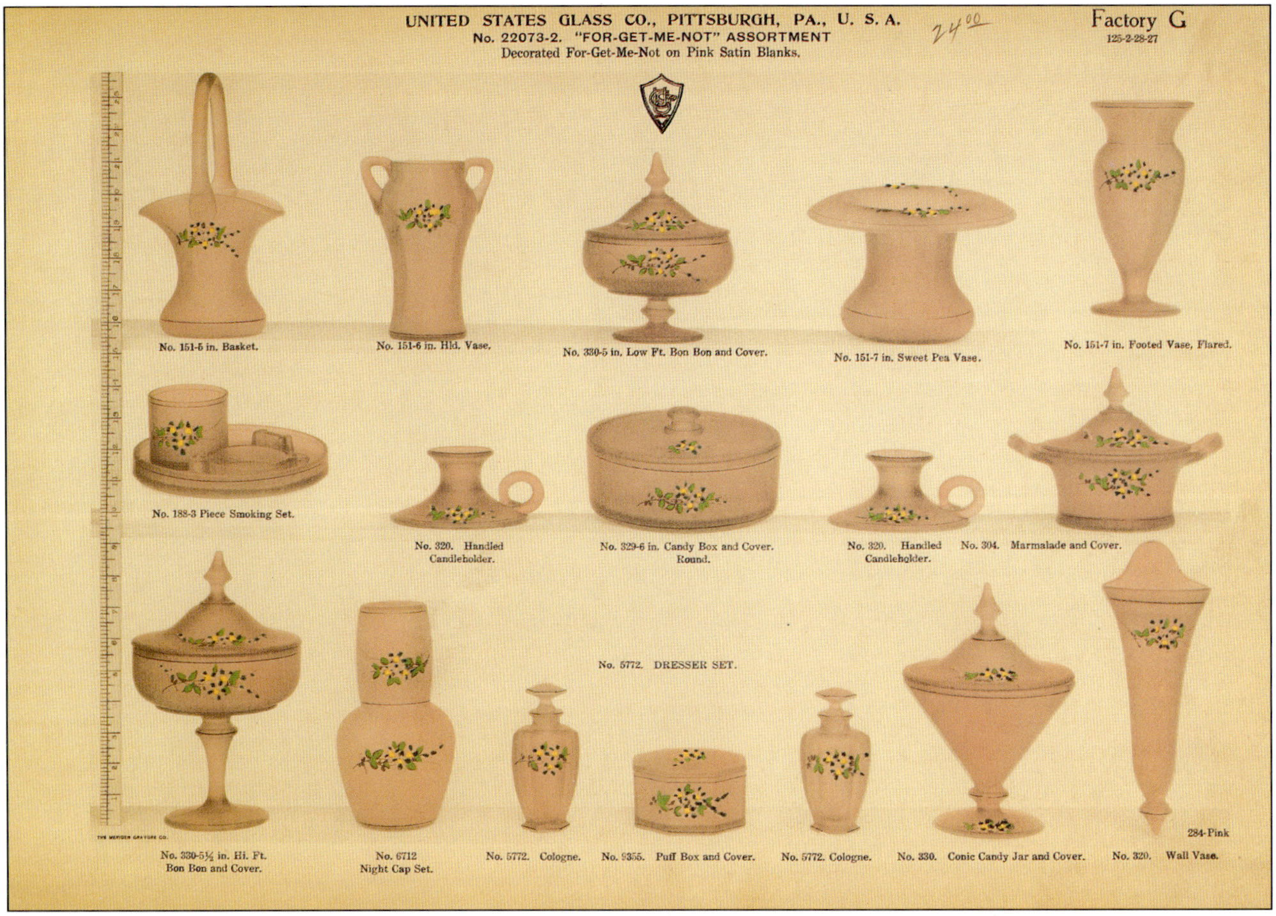

For-Get-Me-Not. 1927 catalog page, Factory G.
Top Row: $65, $55, $55, $45, $45.
Middle Row: $75 set, $65 pair, $55, $55.
Bottom Row: $65, $65 set, $45 each, $45, $65, $115.

Puritan. 1928 catalog page, Factory D.
Top Row: $45, $35, $45, $55.
Middle Row: $45, $55 pair, $45, $45 set.
Bottom Row: $35, $35, $35, $45.

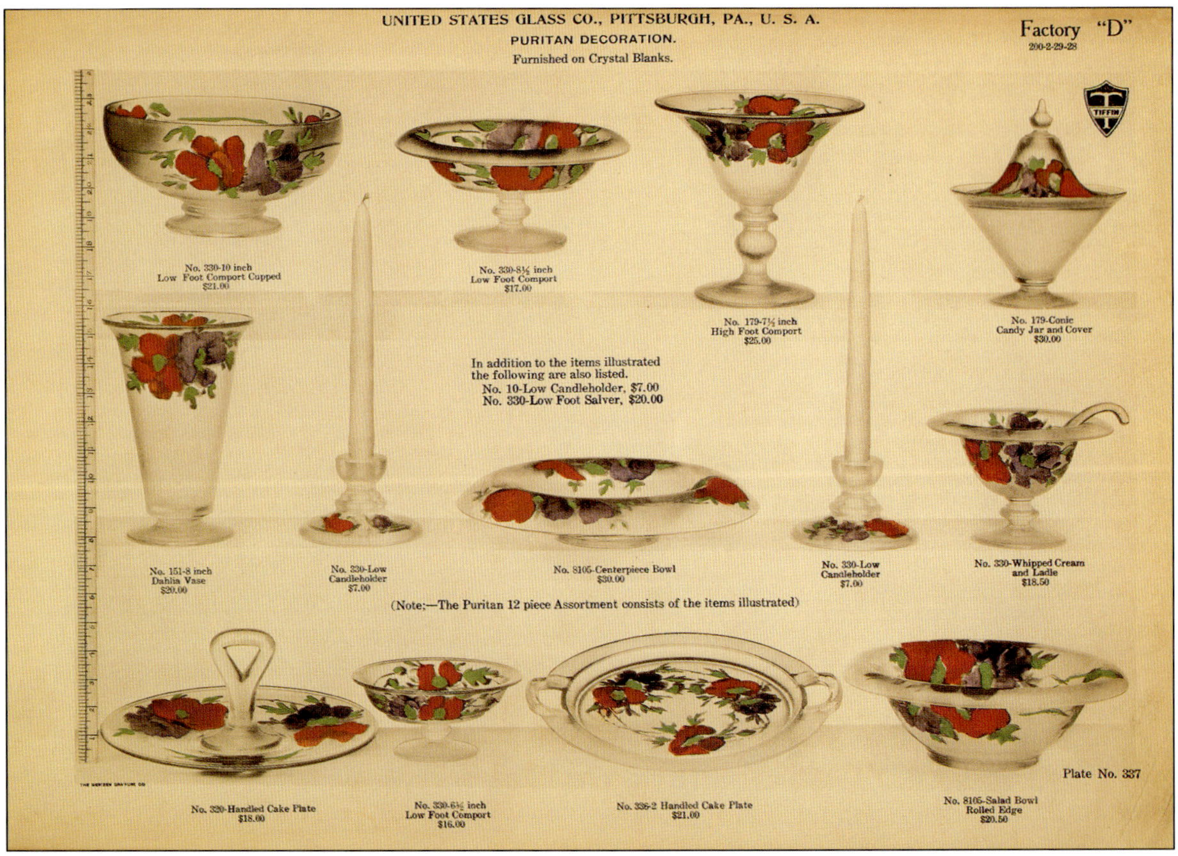

Crystal:
#179, 7.5" High Foot Comport. $35.
#330, 8.5" Low Foot Comport. $35.
Puritan. Crystal #179, 10" Low Foot Comport. $45.
All items were cold painted on crystal blanks and decorated at Factory D. Discontinued in 1929.

No. 607 Decoration. 1927 catalog page, Factory D. Top Row: $35, $55, $55. Middle Row: $45, $45 each, $45. Bottom Row: $35, $45, $45.

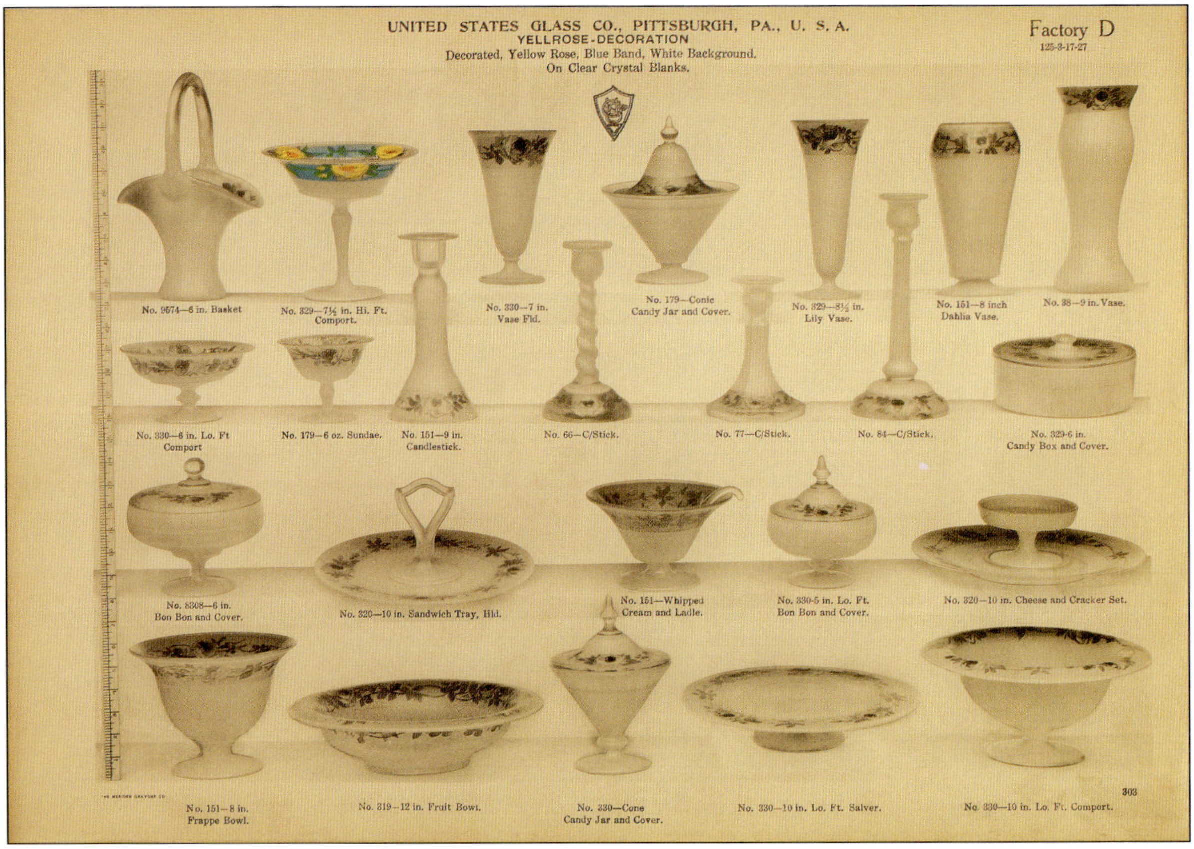

Yellrose. 1927 catalog page, Factory D. Top Row: $55, $45, $35, $55, $45, $45, $45. Upper Middle Row: $35, $25, $30, $30, $30, $30, $45. Lower Middle Row: $45, $35, $35 set, $45, $45 set. Bottom Row: $35, $35, $55, $45, $35.

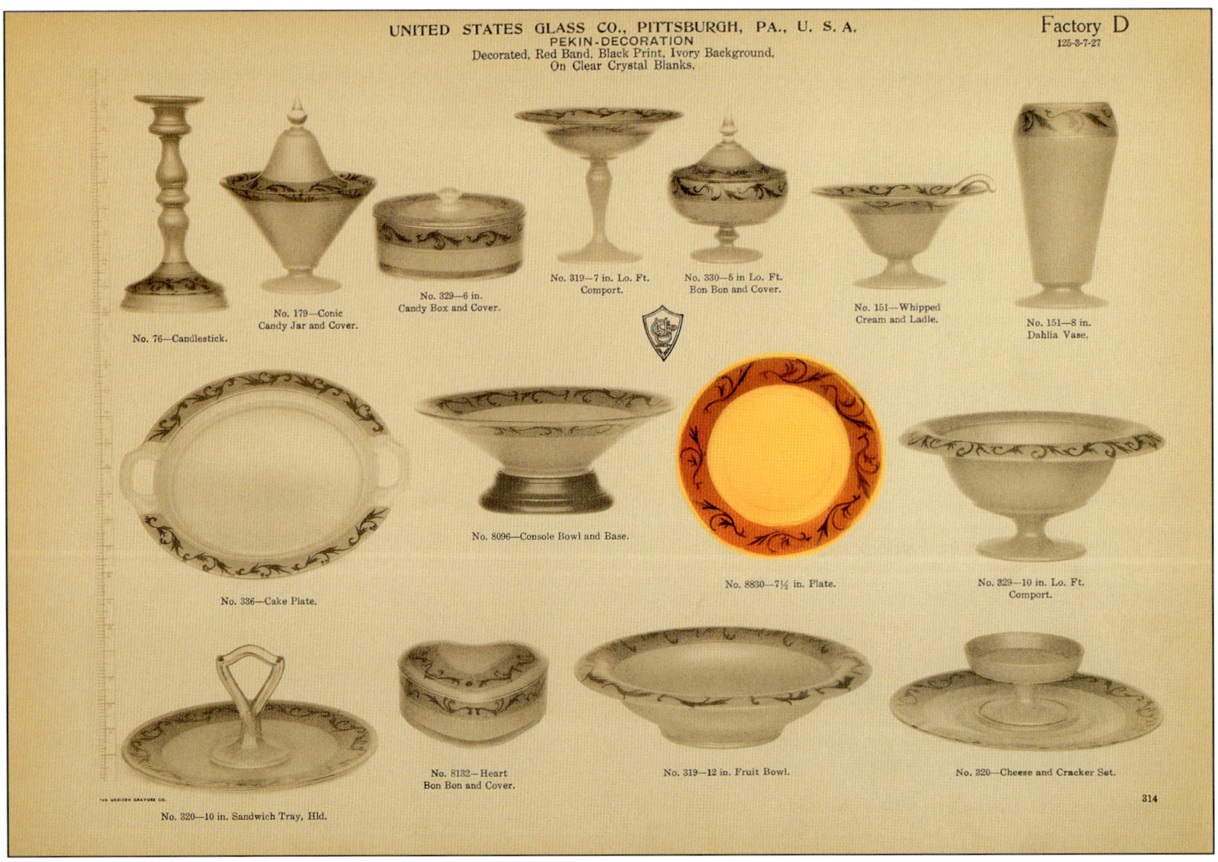

Pekin. 1927 catalog page, Factory D. Top Row: $30, $55, $45, $45, $45, $35 set, $45. Middle Row: $35, $55 set, $10, $35. Bottom Row: $35, $65, $45, $45 set.

Esmeralda. 1927 catalog page, Factory D. Discontinued January 1929.
Top Row: $55, $45, $35, $55, $45, $45.
Upper Middle Row: $35, $25, $30, $30, $30, $45.
Lower Middle Row: $45, $55 set, $45, $45.
Bottom Row: $35, $35, $45, $35.

No. 609 Decoration. 1927 catalog page, Factory D.
Top Row: $45, $40, $30, $35.
Middle Row: $45 each, $45 set.
Bottom Row: $45, $35, $35.

Madrid. 1927 catalog page, Factory D. Top Row: $55, $45, $35, $55, $45, $35, $45. Upper Middle Row: $45, $30, $25, $30, $35, $30, $45. Lower Middle Row: $45, $35, $55 set, $45 set, $35 set. Bottom Row: $45 each.

Venus. c. 1924 catalog page, Factory D. Top Row: $35 set, $20, $45 set, $35, $45. Middle Row: $45 set, $60 pair, $55 set, $35. Bottom Row: $10, $10, $65, $35. The Venus decoration was applied to crystal blanks.

Danube. Undated catalog page, Factory D.
Top Row: $35, $35 set, $45, $45.
Middle Row: $35, $45, $35, $35.
Bottom Row: $45 set, $55 pair, $55 set, $35.
The Danube decoration was applied to crystal blanks.

Tri Color Assortment. 1926 catalog page, Factory D. Top Row: $35, $45, $45 set, $45. Middle Row: $35 set, $55 pair, $55 set, $45. Bottom Row: $45, $35, $45, $35. All decorations are on crystal blanks. The Springtime decoration is on the green-colored pieces, and the Danube decoration on the blue-colored pieces.

Locarno. 1926 catalog page, Factory D.
Top Row: $35, $45, $35, $45.
Middle Row: $45, $45 pair, $45 set, $35 set.
Bottom Row: $35, $35, $35, $45 set.
The Locarno decoration was applied to crystal blanks.

Springtime. c. 1926 catalog page, Factory D.
Top Row: $35, $35 set, $45, $35.
Middle Row: $35, $45, $45, $45.
Bottom Row: $45 set, $55 pair, $45 set, $35.

No. 100 Console Sets. Undated catalog page, Factory D. These are decorated crystal blanks. $55 per set.

Examples of crystal blanks with painted decoration: Orange painted #65, 9.5" h. Candlestick with enameling on base. $35. Yellow painted #66, 7.5" h. Candlestick. $20. Orange painted #151, 9" h. Candlestick with silver overlay decoration. $50. Orange painted #15151, 8" h. Cupped Dahlia Vase with crystal band. $35. Orange was the most prevalent color used to decorate crystal blanks.

The New Glendale

Showing two of the many beautiful and useful pieces furnished in the new Glendale decoration.

A dainty design of pink rose buds and a stippled band of green edged with gold.

UNITED STATES GLASS COMPANY

General Offices and Salesrooms
South Ninth and Bingham Sts. Pittsburgh, Pa.

New York: 1107 Broadway, E. T. W. Craig, Representative
Philadelphia: 10th and Market Sts. J. A. Hemple, Representative
San Francisco: 682 Mission Street, F. M. Dunn, Representative
Boston: 99 Bedford Street, M. A. Lovell, Representative
Los Angeles: 643 South Olive Street, J. F. Stirk, Representative
Dallas: Southland Hotel Building, D. D. Otstott, Inc., Representative
Baltimore: 110 Hopkins Place, John A. Dobson Co., Representative
Chicago: 30 East Randolph Street, F. T. Renshaw, Representative
Denver. 404 Jacobson Building, Norton C. Boyer, Representative
St. Louis: 1017 Olive St., J. Donald Fisher, Representative.

China, Glass and Lamps advertisement, 1924, **Glendale** decoration.

The New Dana Decoration

A decoration of rare beauty consisting of a floral design in gold over a broad band of stippled blue.

Comports, plates, cheese and cracker sets, whipped cream sets, candlesticks and many other useful and decorative pieces.

UNITED STATES GLASS COMPANY

General Offices and Salesrooms
South Ninth and Bingham Sts. Pittsburgh, Pa.

New York: 1107 Broadway, E. T. W. Craig, Representative
Philadelphia: 10th and Market Sts. J. A. Hemple, Representatiye
San Francisco: 682 Mission Street, F. M. Dunn, Representative
Boston: 99 Bedford Street, M. A. Lovell, Representative
Los Angeles: 643 South Olive Street, J. F. Stirk, Representative
Dallas: Southland Hotel Building, D. D. Otstott, Inc., Representative
Baltimore: 110 Hopkins Place, John A. Dobson Co., Representative
Chicago: 30 East Randolph Street, F. T. Renshaw, Representative
Denver. 404 Jacobson Building, Norton C. Boyer, Representative
St. Louis: 1017 Olive St., J. Donald Fisher, Representative.

China, Glass and Lamps advertisement, February 5, 1923, **Dana** decoration.

The Fairfield

The Fairfield decoration is simply beautiful because it is beautifully simple. The body color is either rose or yellow, edged with a heavy black band with two finer bands inside, also in black.

The Fairfield combines dignified design with a vivid dash of color. Furnished in a variety of console sets, candy jars, comports, water sets and sundaes.

UNITED STATES GLASS COMPANY

General Offices and Salesrooms
South Ninth and Bingham Sts. Pittsburgh, Pa.

New York: 1107 Broadway, E. T. W. Craig, Representative
Philadelphia: 10th and Market Sts. J. A. Hemple, Representative
San Francisco: 682 Mission Street, F. M. Dunn, Representative
Boston: 99 Bedford Street, M. A. Lovell, Representative
Los Angeles: 643 South Olive Street, J. F. Stirk, Representative
Dallas: Southland Hotel Building, D. D. Otstott, Inc., Representative
Baltimore: 110 Hopkins Place, John A. Dobson Co., Representative
Chicago: 30 East Randolph Street, F. T. Renshaw, Representative
Denver. 404 Jacobson Building, Norton C. Boyer, Representative
St. Louis: 1017 Olive St., J. Donald Fisher, Representative.

China, Glass and Lamps advertisement, February 16, 1922. The **Fairfield** decoration was applied to crystal blanks.

Attractive Yet Inexpensive Decorated Line

THE item illustrated is typical of a new line of decorated glassware. The decoration is a floral spray in green and white on an amber band, edged with brilliant orange.

This is an inexpensive line, in a variety of shapes, including vases, comports, bowls, etc.

Prices on request, or see it at the Pittsburgh Exhibit.

UNITED STATES GLASS COMPANY
PITTSBURGH, PENNSYLVANIA
OFFICES IN ALL PRINCIPAL CITIES

Visit Our New Display and Sales Rooms—Pottery & Glass Bldg., 954 Liberty Ave., Pittsburgh, Pa.

China, Glass and Lamps advertisement, c. 1925.

Amazon.
White Satin:
#84, 10" h. Candlesticks. $115 pair.
#151, 9" plate. $35.
#179, 9" Low Foot Flared Comport. $50.
#179, 10" Handled Cake Plate. $60.
The Amazon decoration consists of a hand-painted tropical bird perched among branches.

Detail of **Amazon** decoration.

Woodbine. 1927 catalog page, Factory D.
Top Row: $65, $45, $45, $45 set, $50.
Middle Row: $45, $30, $65 set, $45, $45.
Bottom Row: $45, $45, $25, $45.

Woodbine.
White Satin:
#329, 10.5" Low Foot Comport. $45.
#15151, 8" h. Cupped Dahlia Vase. $50.
The Woodbine decoration is similar in appearance to Autumn Leaf. Both designs have a cluster of four leaves connected by gold scrollwork. Decorated at Factory D.

Detail of **Woodbine** decoration.

White Satin:
#76, 8.25" h. Candlesticks. $115 pair.
#8096, 9.5" Console Bowl. $45.
#9574, 10.25" h. x 6" w. Basket. $65.
#84, 10" h. Candlesticks. $115 pair.
#329, 6.25" Whipped Cream. $35.
This unidentified decoration is similar to hand-painted and gold scrollwork designs commonly found on other U. S. Glass decorated white satin blanks.

Detail of unidentified decoration.

White Satin #319, 7.5" High Foot Comport. $35. The unidentified decoration consists of hand-painted pink and orange oriental poppies.

Detail of unidentified oriental poppy decoration.

Jupiter.
White Satin #319, 4" Handled Candlesticks. $60 pair. The Jupiter decoration has a pink or green background with gold latticework on white satin blanks.
White Satin #15151, 8" h. Cupped Dahlia Vase. $65. This decoration consists of white and yellow enameled roses with gold latticework.

Detail of enameled white and yellow roses decoration.

Jupiter. Undated catalog page, Factory D. Top Row: $45, $25, $55, $45, $30, $25. Middle Row: $45 set, $65 pair, $65 set, $45. Bottom Row: $10, $45, $45, $55 set, $45 set.

D-No. 2 Gift Shop Assortment. Undated catalog page, Factory D. Top Row: $65 each, $65 each, $30 each, $25 each. Bottom Row: $35 each, $55, $45, $45, $35 each.

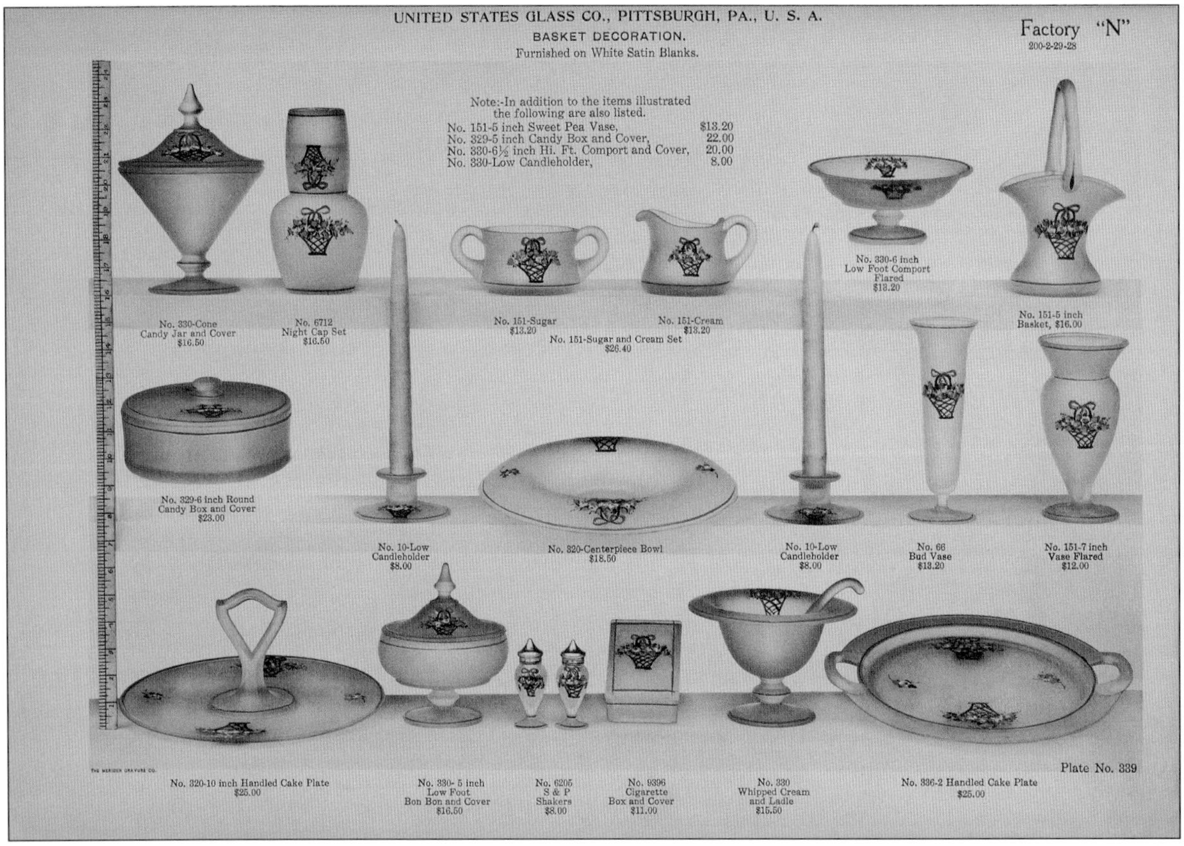

Basket. 1928 catalog page, Factory N.
Top Row: $55, $55 set, $45 set, $35, $55.
Middle Row: $45, $45 pair, $45, $35, $35.
Bottom Row: $40, $45, $45 set, $45, $35 set, $35.
The Basket decoration was also used on pink satin blanks.

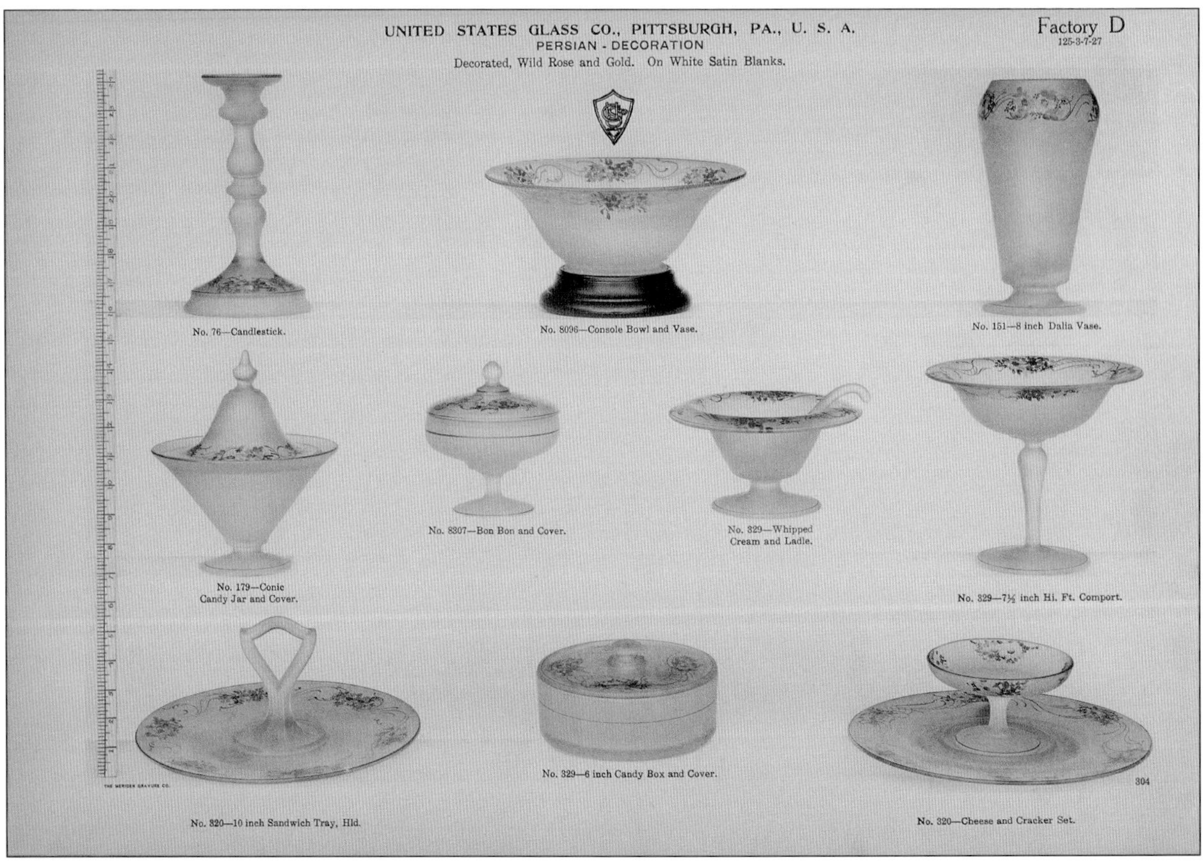

Persian. 1927 catalog page, Factory D.
Top Row: $55, $65 set, $65.
Middle Row: $65, $55, $45 set, $45.
Bottom Row: $45, $45, $55 set.

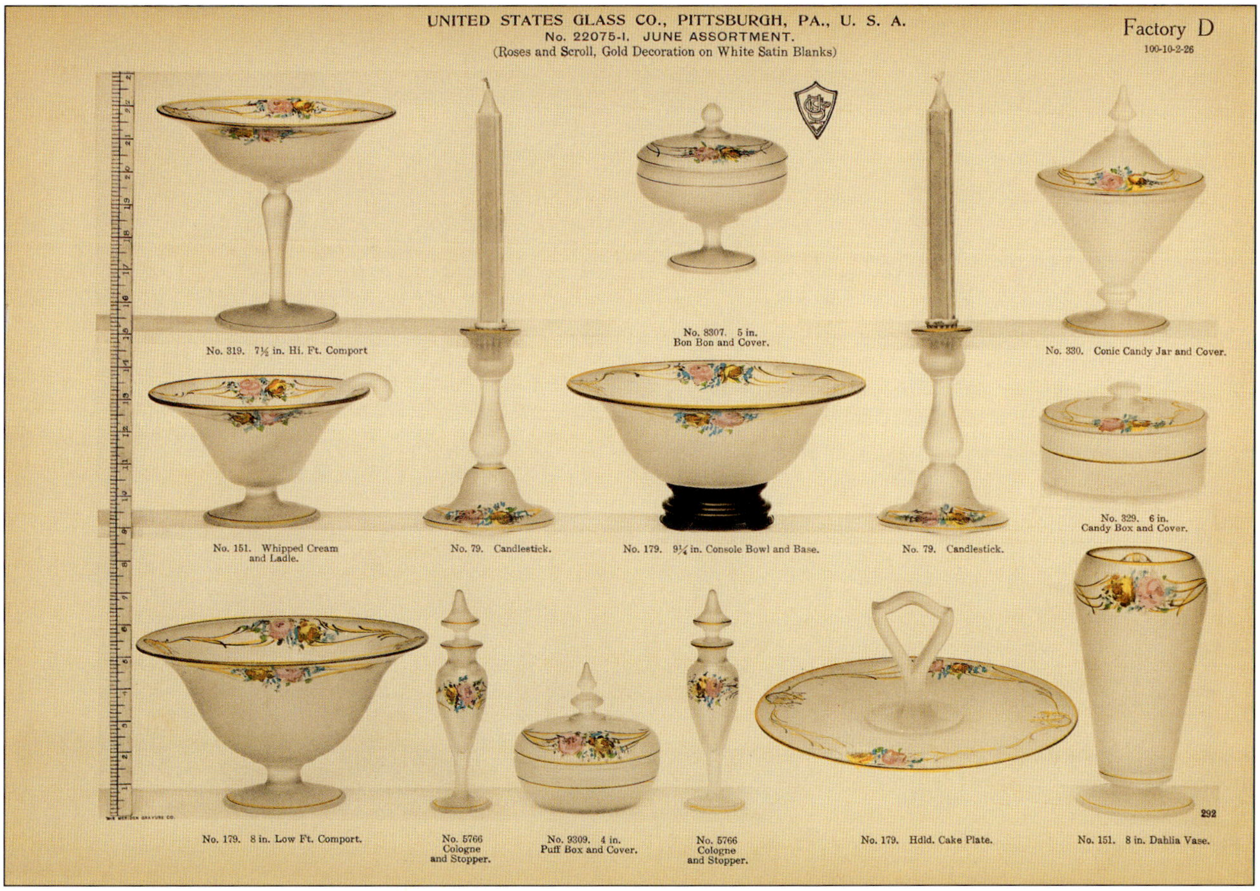

June. 1926 catalog page, Factory D.
Top Row: $45, $45, $65.
Middle Row: $45 set, $75 pair, $65 set, $55.
Bottom Row: $45, $65 each, $55, $45, $55.

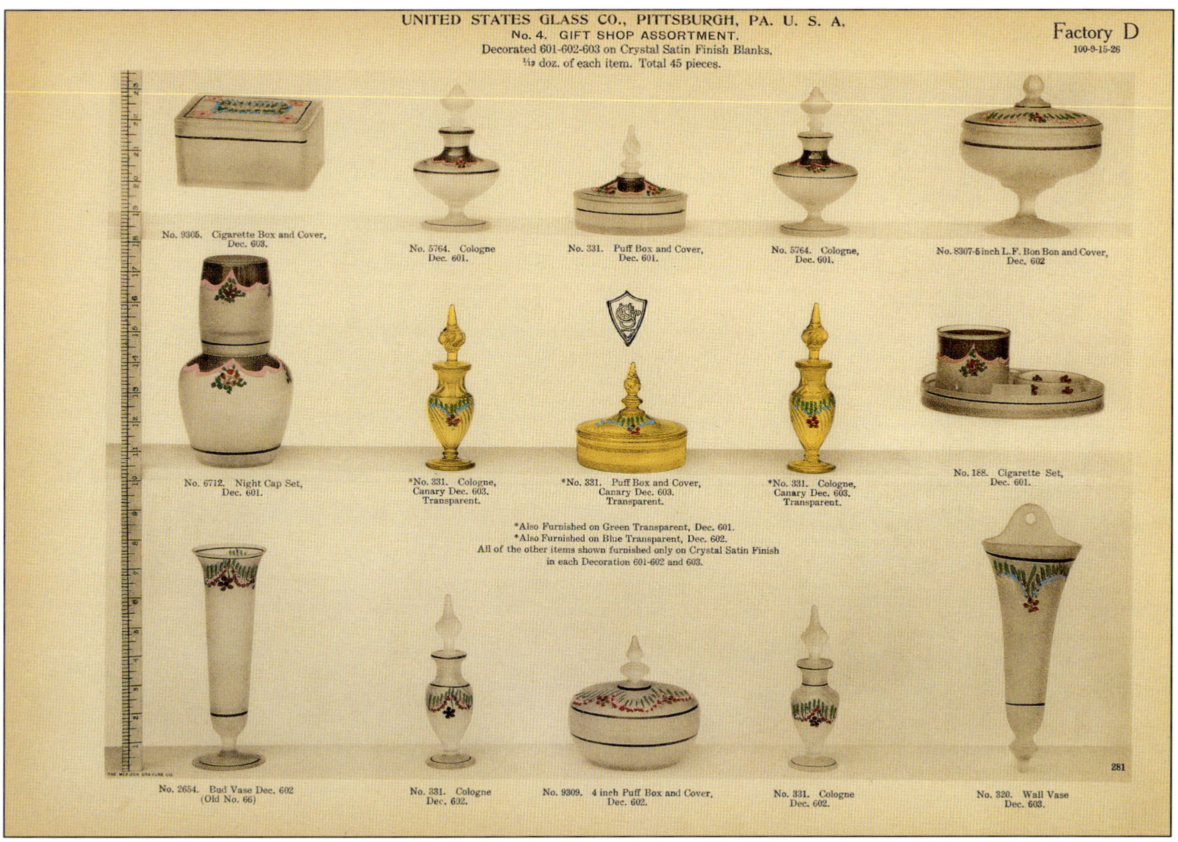

No. 4 Gift Shop Assortment. 1926 catalog page, Factory D.
Top Row: $45, $65 each, $45, $45.
Middle Row: $65 set, $75 each, $55, $75 set.
Bottom Row: $45, $65 each, $45, $95.

Primrose.
c. 1927 catalog page, Factory D.
Top Row: $45, $25, $55, $45, $30, $25.
Middle Row: $45 set, $65 pair, $65 set, $45.
Bottom Row: $10, $45, $45, $55 set, $45 set.

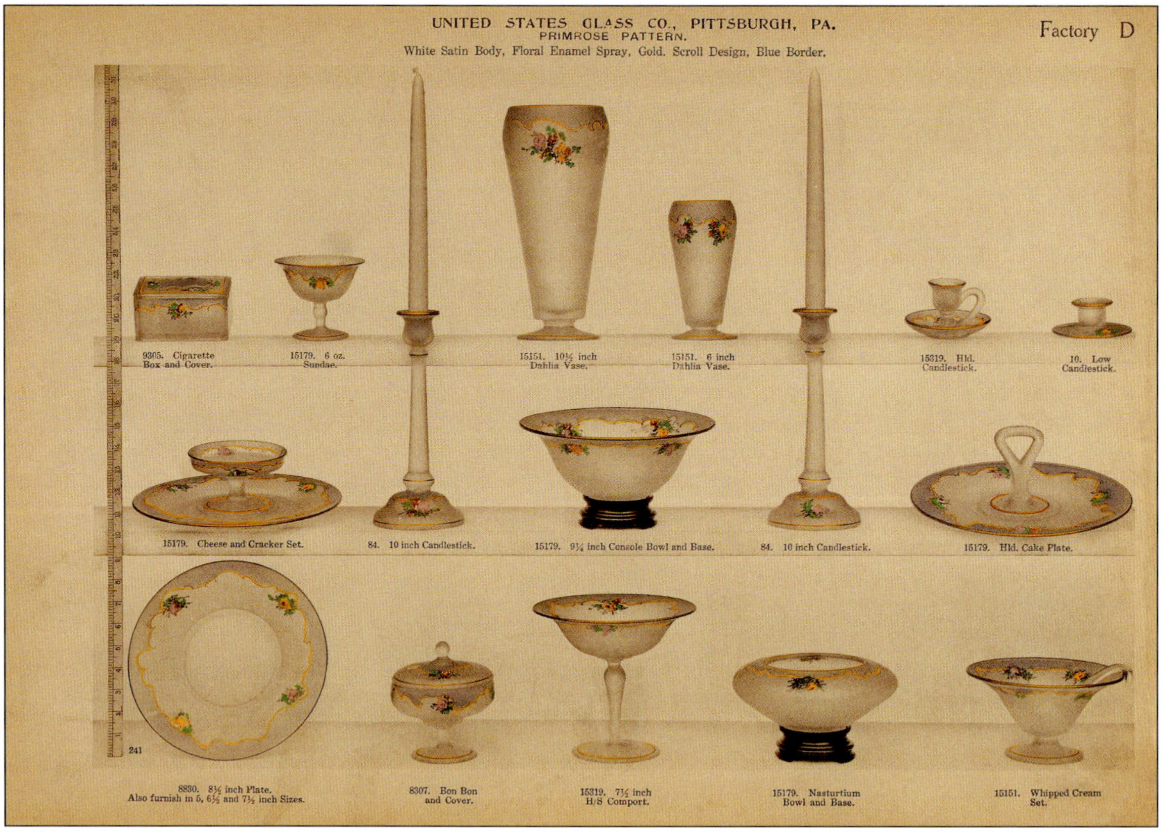

UNITED STATES GLASS CO., PITTSBURGH, PA.
PRIMROSE PATTERN.
White Satin Body, Floral Enamel Spray, Gold. Scroll Design, Blue Border.

Factory D

9305. Cigarette Box and Cover.
15179. 6 oz. Sundae.
15151. 10½ inch Dahlia Vase.
15151. 6 inch Dahlia Vase.
15319. Hld. Candlestick.
10. Low Candlestick.
15179. Cheese and Cracker Set.
84. 10 inch Candlestick.
15179. 9¼ inch Console Bowl and Base.
84. 10 inch Candlestick.
15179. Hld. Cake Plate.
241
8830. 8½ inch Plate. Also furnish in 5, 6½ and 7½ inch Sizes.
8307. Bon Bon and Cover.
15319. 7½ inch H/S Comport.
15179. Nasturtium Bowl and Base.
15151. Whipped Cream Set.

White Satin:
#15151, 10" h. Cupped Dahlia Vase, $85.
#444, 12 oz. Ice Tea Tumbler, $25.
#6461, 2 qt. Ice Tea Jug, $275.
Only known on white satin blanks.

China, Glass and Lamps advertisement, June 8, 1925.

Jungle Assortment. 1927 catalog page, Factory N.
Top Row: $65, $45, $55, $45, $45.
Middle Row: $55, $75 pair, $55, $75 set.
Bottom Row: $45, $65, $45 each, $45, $55, $125.

Jungle Assortment. 1927 catalog page, Factory N.
Top Row: $65, $45, $55, $45, $45.
Middle Row: $55, $75 pair, $55, $75 set.
Bottom Row: $45, $65, $45 each, $45, $55, $125.

No. 14 Parrot.
Green Satin #330:
5" Candlesticks. $75 pair.
8.75" h. High Foot Bon Bon and Cover. $65.
6" h. Low Foot Bon Bon and Cover. $55.
8" h. Conic Candy Jar and Cover. $55.
The No. 14 Parrot is often misidentified as Jungle or Jungle Assortment. As shown on the catalog page, the collection was offered as the No. 22052 Jungle Assortment. When offered singly, it was known as the No. 14 Parrot. Introduced c. 1925, No. 14 Parrot was also offered on pink satin blanks.

No. 14 Parrot.
Green Satin:
#329, 6.25" Candy Box and Cover. $55.
#188, 3 Piece Smoking Set, 6.25" Tray, 4" Ash Tray, 2.5" Round Cigarette Holder. $75 set.
#329, 5.25" Candy Box and Cover. $55.
The No. 14 Parrot decoration is often found in worn condition because the design was cold painted (not fired).

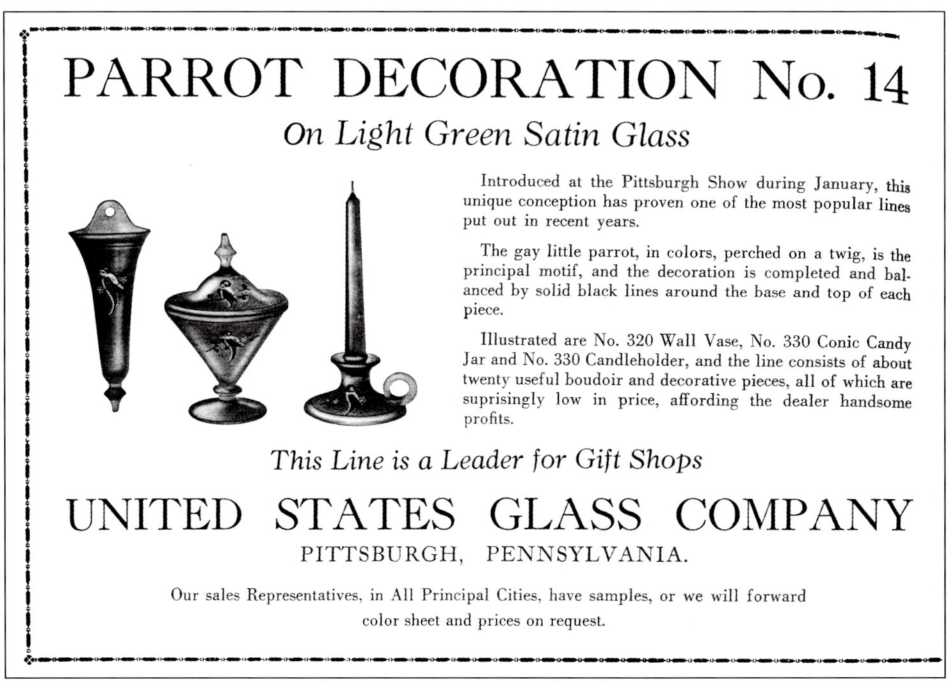

PARROT DECORATION No. 14

On Light Green Satin Glass

Introduced at the Pittsburgh Show during January, this unique conception has proven one of the most popular lines put out in recent years.

The gay little parrot, in colors, perched on a twig, is the principal motif, and the decoration is completed and balanced by solid black lines around the base and top of each piece.

Illustrated are No. 320 Wall Vase, No. 330 Conic Candy Jar and No. 330 Candleholder, and the line consists of about twenty useful boudoir and decorative pieces, all of which are suprisingly low in price, affording the dealer handsome profits.

This Line is a Leader for Gift Shops

UNITED STATES GLASS COMPANY

PITTSBURGH, PENNSYLVANIA.

Our sales Representatives, in All Principal Cities, have samples, or we will forward color sheet and prices on request.

China, Glass and Lamps advertisement, c. 1925, **No. 14 Parrot** decoration.

China, Glass and Lamps advertisement, May 4, 1925, **Parakeet Twins** decoration.

Parakeet Twins.
Canary Satin #6205, 3.5" h. Salt and Pepper Shakers. $45. The Parakeet Twins design is very similar in appearance to the No. 14 Parrot, which has the parrot perched on a flowering branch. The Parakeet Twins design has the parakeet on a wire hoop. An advertisement for the Parakeet Twins claims that the design was also available on green, blue, and white satin blanks.

Parakeet Twins.
Crystal with orange paint #2629, 6" h. Vase. $25.
Crystal with orange and lavender paint #6712, 5.75" Night Cap Sets, minus tumblers. $25 each.
The two styles of candlesticks are New Martinsville Glass Company products with the same decoration.

China, Glass and Lamps advertisement, January 12, 1925, shows another type of salt and pepper shaker.

Yellow Daisy. 1927 catalog page, Factory N.
Top Row: $65, $45, $45 set, $45, $45 set, $45, $45.
Upper Middle Row: $45, $65 pair, $45, $75 set.
Lower Middle Row: $45 each, $45.
Bottom Row: $55, $65 set, $45 each, $45, $55, $125.

Mum. 1927 catalog page, Factory D.
Top Row: $65, $55, $45, $45, $45, $45.
Upper Middle Row: $45, $45, $45, $30, $75 set.
Lower Middle Row: $45.
Bottom Row: $55, $65 set, $45 each, $45, $55, $125.
The Mum decoration was also painted on pink satin blanks.

Bridal. 1926 catalog page, Factory D.
Top Row: $65, $15, $55 set, $65.
Middle Row: $55, $125 pair, $55, $45 set.
Bottom Row: $45, $125 pair, $65 set, $45.

For-Get-Me-Not. 1926 catalog page, Factory G.
Top Row: $55, $45, $45, $45, $45.
Middle Row: $75 set, $65 pair, $45, $45.
Bottom Row: $55, $65 set, $45 each, $45, $55, $125.

Poppy. 1926 catalog page, Factory D.
Top Row: $55, $45, $45, $45, $45.
Middle Row: $75 set, $65 pair, $45, $45.
Bottom Row: $55, $65 set, $45 each, $45, $55, $125.

China, Glass and Lamps advertisement, November 11, 1926, **For-Get-Me-Not** decoration. Also found on pink satin blanks.

Cosmo. 1927 catalog page, Factory D.
Top Row: $55, $45, $45, $45, $45, $45.
Upper Middle Row: $45, $35, $45, $30, $75 set.
Lower Middle Row: $45.
Bottom Row: $55, $65 set, $45 each, $45, $55, $125.

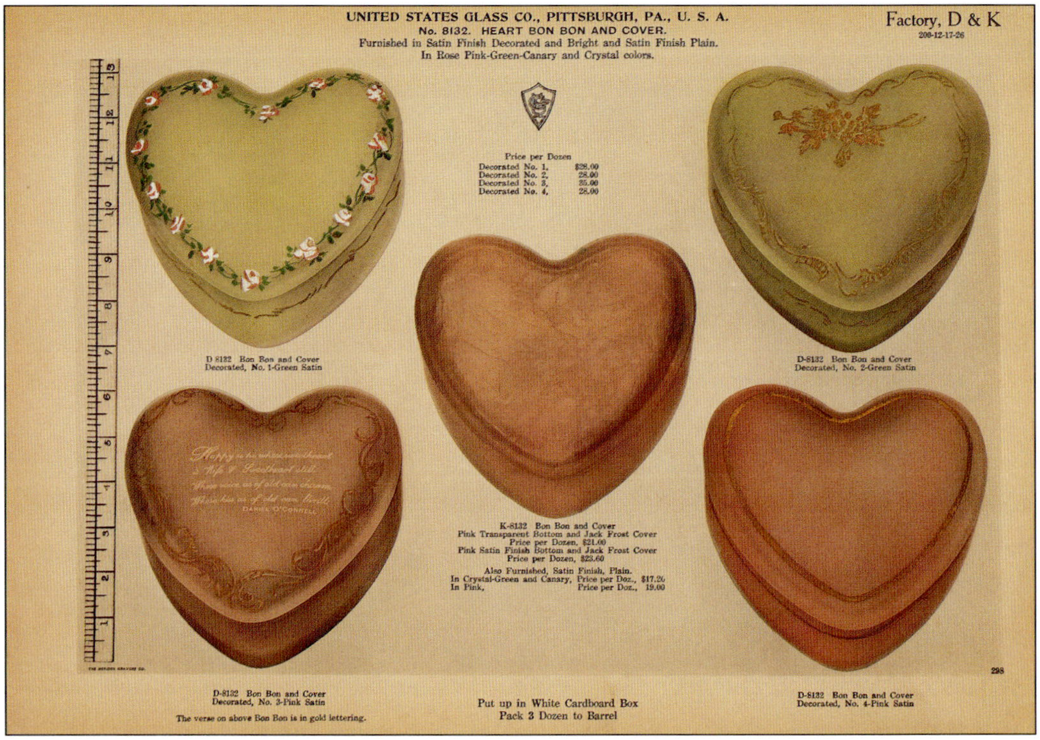

Heart Bon Bon and Cover. 1926 catalog page, Factories D and K. Top Row: $135, $125. Middle Row: $155. Bottom Row: $135, $125. The blanks were made at Factory K and decorated at Factory D. The verse on the lower left side bon bon reads, "Happy is he whose sweetheart is wife and sweetheart still, whose voice as of old can charm, whose kiss as of old can thrill." Daniel O. O'Connell.

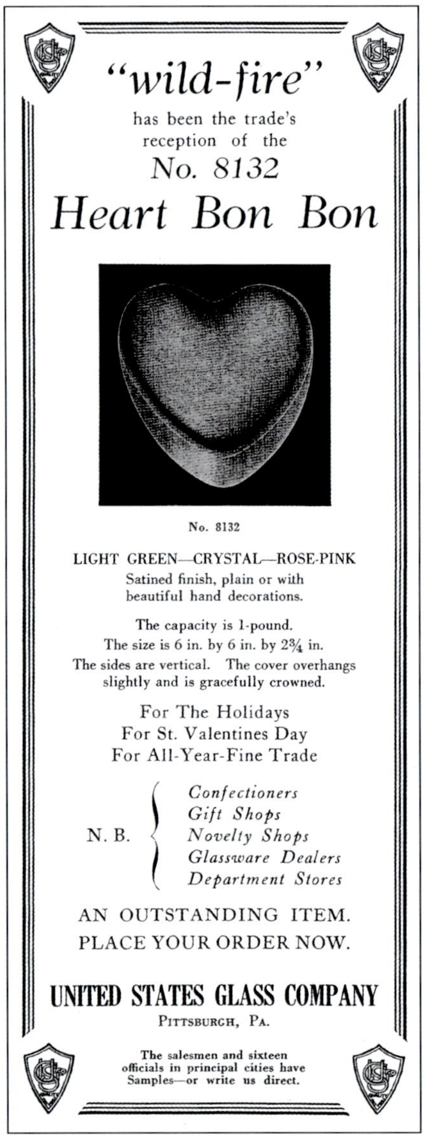

China, Glass and Lamps advertisement, October 18, 1926, #8132 Heart Bon Bon in green, crystal, or pink colors.

Decorated Night Cap Set Assortment. 1926 catalog page, Factory D.
Top Row: $55 each.
Bottom Row: $65 each.

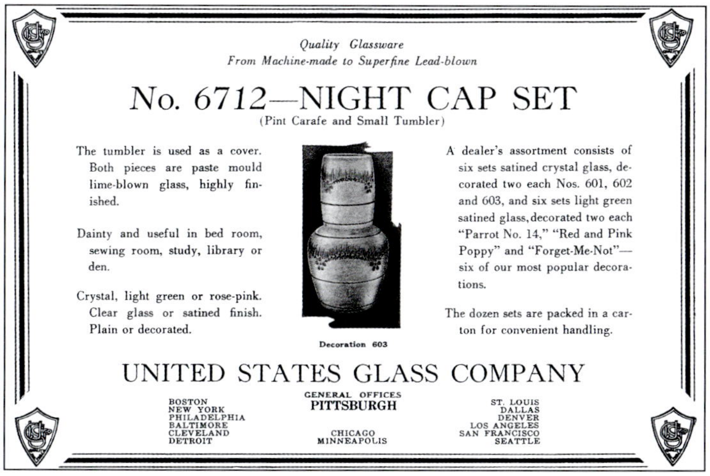

China, Glass and Lamps advertisement, November 8, 1926.

Green Satin #15310:
9" Low Foot Comport. $55.
10.25" h. x 6" w. Basket. $75.
This unidentified U. S. Glass decoration is very similar in appearance to the Autumn Leaf and Woodbine designs. Found on green satin #15310 blanks.

Detail of decoration.

Green #111, 12" h. Egyptian Vase, **Lattice** decoration. $135. The upper and lower portions of the vase have a satin finish, while the middle section has a bright finish with gold criss-crossing lines. This creates a trellis or lattice effect. Blown and decorated at Factory R.

D-No. 1 Gift Shop Assortment. Undated catalog page, Factory D.
The **Minorca** decoration is a gold-painted design.
Top Row: $25, $75, $45, $55, $30.
Middle Row: $65, $55 pair, $55 set, $65.
Bottom Row: $45, $55 set, $45 set.

Tropical.
Black Satin:
#15151, 8" h. Cupped Dahlia Vase. $55.
#179, 10" Handled Cake Plate. $45.
The Tropical decoration is a painted white-gold design of a bird perched on a flowering branch.

Detail of **Tropical** decoration.

Chapter 2

Gold Decorations

Detail of **Damascus** decoration.

Damascus.
Black Satin #320, 9" h. Wall Vase. $225.
The Damascus decoration has a gold-painted palm frond and a band of painted blocks in alternating colors of rust and turquoise against a bright black background. The lower portion of the wall vase has a satin finish. Decorated at Factory D.

Rajah.
Black Satin #16261, 8.5" h. Open Work Flower Arranger Vase. $85. The No. 22030 Rajah decoration is a gold rubber stamp design on black satin blanks. Decorated at Factory D and discontinued in February 1929.

Detail of **Rajah** design.

Rajah. 1927 catalog page, Factory D.
Top Row: $75, $75 pair, $55, $65.
Middle Row: $65, $75, $65, $85.
Bottom Row: $55, $100 pair, $65 set, $75.

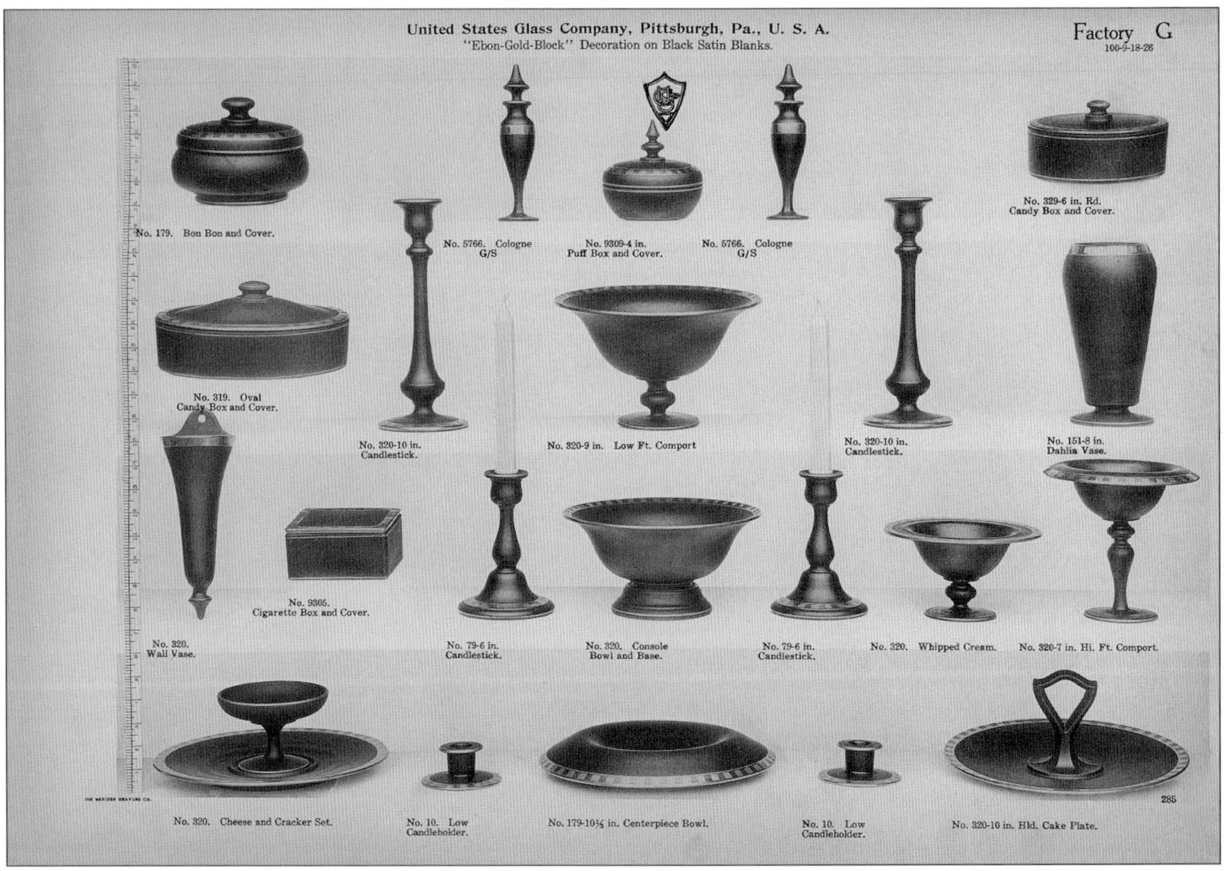

Ebon-Gold-Block. 1927 catalog page, Factory G.
Top Row: $65, $115 each, $65, $75.
Upper Middle Row: $75, $115 pair, $65, $75.
Lower Middle Row: $145, $65, $95 pair, $75 set, $55, $65.
Bottom Row: $55 set, $70 pair, $55, $55.

Ebon-Gold-Block.
Black Satin:
#15151, 8" h. Cupped Dahlia Vase. $75.
#10, 3.75" Low Candleholder. $35.
The Ebon-Gold-Block decoration consists of alternating matte and burnished gold blocks in a band .75" wide on black satin blanks.

Detail of **Ebon-Gold-Block** decoration.

Gold Line Decoration No. 1. c. 1924 catalog page, Factory GED.
Top Row: $65, $85, $85 set, $155.
Middle Row: $65, $130 pair, $85, $45 set.
Bottom Row: $115, $175 pair, $115, $125.

Gold Line Decoration No. 1. c. 1924 catalog page, Factory GED.
Top Row: $55, $55, $135, $145, $65, $115.
Middle Row: $95, $115 pair, $65, $65 set.
Bottom Row: $85 set, $110 pair, $85 set, $65, $65.

Gold Line Decoration No. 1.
Royal Blue Satin:
#15320, 10.25" Handled Sandwich Tray. $65.
#15179, 10" Two Handled Console Bowl. $115.
#15179, 4.75" Whipped Cream. $65.
Satin Blanks were decorated with Gold Line Decoration No. 1, which consists of two wide gold bands and one thin gold band on a bright finish background. Also found on black satin blanks.

Gold Line Decoration No. 1.
Royal Blue Satin:
#8098, 7.5" Footed Rose Bowl. $115.
#15319, 6.5" h. Two Handled Vase. $85.
#15179, 10" Urn Vase. $115.
#15320, 7" h. High Foot Comport. $85.
The #15319 two handled vase was also available in a 10" size.

Gold Line Decoration No. 1.
Royal Blue Satin:
Unidentified line number, 6.5" h. Hot Weather Candles. $350 pair.
#15320, 10" h. Candlestick. $65.
#76, 8.5" h. Candlestick. $65.
#79, 6" h. Candlestick. $55.
The #15320 and #76 candlesticks hold hot weather candles. These glass candles are square with a round base and can be found in blue, canary, black, amethyst, royal blue, jasper, agate blend, and onyx blend.

No. 8105 Console Sets. Undated catalog page, Factory G. Top Row: $100 set, $80 set. Middle Row: $100 set, $125 set, $125 set. Bottom Row: $100 per set.

Gold Encrustations D and E. Undated catalog page, Factory GED. Gold Encrustation D is similar in design to the Melrose gold band commonly found on Tiffin Glass stemware. Gold Encrustation E resembles two, back-to-back, cursive "C's." Top Row: $75, $110 pair, $75 set, $65, $65. Middle Row: $125, $130 pair, $65, $115. Bottom Row: $65, $145, $165, $15, $15.

UNITED STATES GLASS CO., PITTSBURGH, PA.

Factory G. E. D.

GOLD ENCRUSTATIONS D AND E.
ON BRIGHT BLACK AND ROYAL BLUE COLORS.

8105. 10 inch Fld. Console Bowl and Base Black Glass Enc. "D"

15320. 10¼ inch Cheese and Cracker Set Black Glass Enc. "E"

8098. 7½ inch Ftd. Rose Bowl. Royal Blue Enc. "E"

15179. Ftd. Bon Bon and Cover. Black Glass Enc. "D"

15320. 10¼ inch Hld. Sandwich Tray. Black Glass Enc. "E"

15179. 10 inch 2 Hld. Candlestick. Black Glass Enc. "D"

15179. 10 inch 2 Hld. Console Bowl. Black Glass Enc. "D"

15179. 10 inch 2 Hld. Candlestick. Black Glass Enc. "D"

15320. 10¼ inch Ftd. and Hld. Sandwich Tray Black Glass Enc. "D"

247

15320. 10¼ inch. Ftd. Cheese and Cracker Set with Cover. Royal Blue Glass. Enc. "E"

8098. 10 inch Fld. and Ftd. Console Bowl. Royal Blue Glass Enc. "D"

15179. 8 inch Cupped Comport. Black Glass Enc. "D"

8098. 11 inch Ftd. Orange Bowl. Black Glass, Gold Enc. "E"

15319. 6½ inch 2 Hld. Vase. Black Glass Enc. "D"

Gold Encrustations D and E. Undated catalog page, Factory GED.
Top Row: $75 set, $55 set, $85, $155.
Middle Row: $65, $165 pair, $125, $95.
Bottom Row: $135, $85, $65, $75 set, $65.

Detail of gold encrusted band.

Ritz Carlton.
Royal Blue #74, 10" h. candlesticks with gold encrusted band. $130 pair.

Canary Satin #15315, 7" High Foot Comport with gold band. $75.
Blue Satin #15320, 9" Low Foot Comport with unidentified gold band. $55.
Only the canary comport is part of the Ritz Carlton assortment.

Detail of gold band on canary comport.

Detail of unidentified gold band on blue comport.

Ritz Carlton.
Red Satin #179, 10" Handled Cake Plate. $55.
Blue Satin #74, 10" h. Candlestick. $65.
Both items have the identical gold encrusted band. The cake plate also has a textured stipple finish that was given to some items in the Ritz Carlton line. Further information can be found in *Tiffin Glassmasters, Book II* by Fred Bickenheuser.

Detail of stipple finish and gold band.

Royal Blue Satin #15179, 8.25" h. Footed Bon Bon with unidentified gold band. $155.

Detail of unidentified gold band.

Colored Vases – Gold Encrusted. Undated catalog page, Factory R.
$45, $55, $65, $65.

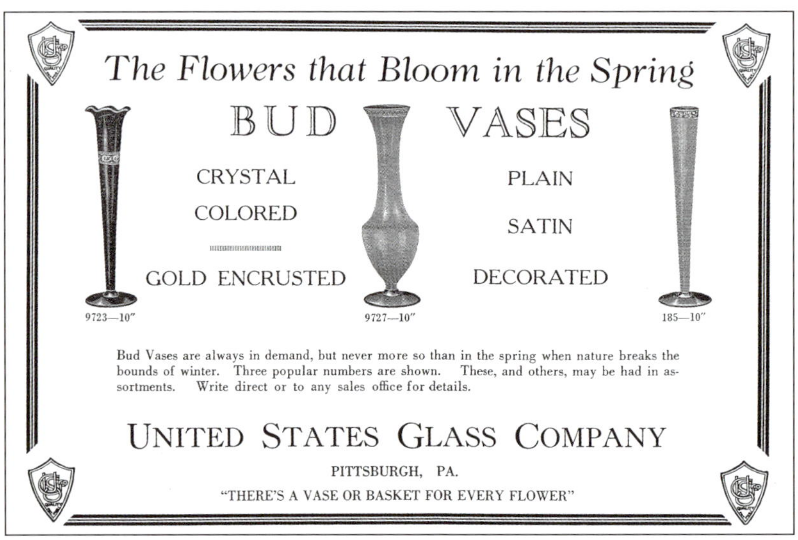

China, Glass and Lamps advertisement,
March 28, 1927.

Chapter 3

Bright with Satin Finish

Beeswax and hydrofluoric acid were used to create the bright with satin finish decorations. A pattern utilizing beeswax was applied to glass objects prior to immersion in a hydrofluoric acid bath. The unprotected glass reacted with the acid to produce a satin finish. The beeswax was removed in a hot water bath to expose the pattern.

Echec. Undated catalog page, Factory G.
Top Row: $125 set, $175 each, $135, $115.
Upper Middle Row: $135.
Lower Middle Row: $135, $105, $105.
Bottom Row: $95 set, $135 pair, $95 set, $95.

Echec.
Black Satin:
#15319, 12" Rolled Edge Fruit Bowl. $75.
#15151, 10" h. Cupped Dahlia Vase. $115.
#15320, 10" h. Candlesticks. $135 pair.
The Echec decoration is a series of satin and bright squares in a checkered pattern. It was introduced in 1925 and is only found on black.

Echec.
Black Satin:
#15179, 10" h. 1/2 lb. Candy Jar and Cover. $125.
#15179, 8" Cupped Comport. $95.
Unidentified line number, 4.25" Low Candleholders. $125 pair.
#79, 6" h. Candlesticks. $125 pair.

Echec.
Black Satin:
#15179, 10" h. Footed Bon Bon and Cover. $135.
#15319, 10" h. Handled Vase. $65.
#8098, 7.5" Footed Rose Bowl. $145.

Echec.
Black Satin, unidentified line number, 5.5" Cigarette Holder. $225.

December 28, 1925. CHINA, GLASS AND LAMPS Fifteen

See These New Items

At The

Pittsburgh Glass Exhibit

It's a habit now, with hundreds of buyers to drop in at 954 Liberty Ave., the permanent exhibit of the United States Glass Co., every time they come to Pittsburgh. They know that here they will find the latest in glassware, the last word in designs and decorations, and ideas that can be found nowhere else.

Nineteen twenty-six promises to be a big year for those who depend on foresight for success. Be sure to see what United States Glass Co. can offer you at the Pittsburgh Show in January.

United States Glass Co.
Pittsburgh, Pa.

Look for the Gold *Seal of Quality*

No. 9352 Book Ends

A-24 Dainty Boudoir Lamp "Pat. App. For"

"Slick" Sugar Dispenser "Pat. App. For"

No. 9309 Ribbon Decorated Vanity Set

No. 16261 8½ in. Flower Holder Echec's Decoration "Pat. App. For"

No. 9354 Smokers Tray "Pat. App. For"

No. 15319 Oval Bon Bon Box and Cover

SALES OFFICES IN ALL LARGE CITIES

China, Glass and Lamps advertisement, December 28, 1925.

New Echec's Glassware— A Fine Holiday Line

IN THIS decoration we have achieved the unusual by combining both satin and brilliant finish in a bold square pattern edged with gold bands. The items illustrated are typical of the line, which is wide and includes pieces that are particularly suitable for the Holiday trade and many others that will find use in practically every room in the home.

Write for illustrations and prices on the complete line.

Echec's Pattern on Comport

Echec's Pattern 16261 Flower Holder.

(PAT. APPL. FOR)

UNITED STATES GLASS COMPANY
PITTSBURGH, PENNA.
SALES OFFICES IN ALL LARGE CITIES

"Visit Our Permanent Exhibit at 954 Liberty Avenue when in Pittsburgh"

China, Glass and Lamps advertisement, November 30, 1925.

Kimberly.
Ruby Satin:
#330, 9.75" Low Foot Flared Comport. $200.
#330, 7" h. Flared Vase. $215.
#79, 6" h. Candlesticks. $275 pair.
The Kimberly decoration consists of bright finish intersecting lines in a diamond grid with a satin finish background. The decoration was named Kimberly after the world's greatest diamond mine. It was introduced c.1925.

Kimberly.
Ruby Satin:
#15320, 10" h. Candlesticks. $300 pair.
#16261, 8.5" h. Open Work Flower Arranger Vase. $345.

Kimberly.
Ruby Satin #8098, 7" Footed Rose Bowl. $315.

Kimberly.
Ruby Satin:
#330, 8" h. Cone Candy Jar and Cover. $350.
#15320, 10.5" Handled Cake Plate. $225.
#15320 Cheese and Cracker Set with 10" plate and 4.5" cheese comport. $225 set.

China, Glass and Lamps advertisement, July 12, 1926.

Kimberly.
Black Satin:
#15319, 10" h. Two Handled Vase. $165.
#320, 9" h. Wall Vase. $215.
#15179, 9.5" h. 1/2 lb. Candy Jar and Cover. $165.
#330, 5" Low Foot Bon Bon and Cover. $155.

Kimberly.
Black Satin:
#79, 6" h. Candlesticks. $135 pair.
#320, 9" Console Bowl. $85.

UNITED STATES GLASS CO., PITTSBURGH, PA., U. S. A.
SATIN RIBBON DECORATION
FURNISHED ON BLACK GLASS

Factory G

No. 15151
10½ inch Dahlia Vase
Cupped

No. 15179. ½ lb.
Candy Jar and Cover

No. 9305. Cigarette Box and Cover

No. 15320. Wall Vase

No. 16261. 8½ inch
Flower Holder

No. 15320
Ftd. Cheese and Cracker Set

No. 15319. 10 inch Hld. Vase

No. 15320. 9 inch Low Ft. Comport

No. 15179. 8 inch Comport
Cupped

No. 79. 6 inch Candlestick

No. 15320
9 inch Console Bowl and Base

No. 79. 6 inch Candlestick

No. 8098. 7½ inch Ftd. Rose Bowl

265

Ribbon. c. 1925 catalog page, Factory G.
Top Row: $95, $165, $145, $215, $115.
Middle Row: $185, $165, $95.
Bottom Row: $75, $125 pair, $95 set, $115.

Ribbon.
Black Satin:
#9309, 4" Puff Box and Cover. $175.
#8098, 7" Footed Rose Bowl. $145.
#10, 3.75" Low Candle Holder. $45.
#319, 8.5" Oval Candy Box and Cover. $165.
Ribbon was introduced in 1925 and produced at Factory G. The decoration consists of alternating bright and satin stripes.

Ribbon.
Black Satin:
#79, 6" h. Candlesticks. $125 pair.
#15179, 10" Tourraine Comport. $75.

Ribbon.
Black Satin:
#16261, 8.5" h. Open Work Flower Arranger Vase. $115.
#15151, 6" h. Cupped Dahlia Vase. $75.

China, Glass, and Lamps advertisement for the **Ribbon** line.

Diamond Block.
Black Satin:
#8177, 5" Low Candleholders. $115 pair.
#15320, 7" High Foot Comport. $75.
This design is comprised of a series of five bright diamonds stacked in a snowflake-like pattern on a satin background. A 1920s U. S. Glass inventory lists a Diamond Block design.

Detail of **Diamond Block** design.

Black Satin #15151, 6" h. Cupped Dahlia Vase with unidentified decoration. $75. The decoration consists of shiny black looping ribbons on a black satin background.

Detail of diamond band design.

Black:
#320 Cheese and Cracker Set with 10" plate and 4.5" cheese comport. $95 set.
#10, 3.75" Low Candleholders. $85 pair.
#179, 10.5" Rolled Edge Table Center Bowl with #9320, 5.75" base. $75.
The unidentified decoration is comprised of a band of satin diamonds on a bright black background.

Chapter 4

Etched and Cut Decorations

Poppae. 1928 catalog page, Factory G. A pattern that is difficult to find.
Top Row: $95, $45, $135, $95, $65, $95.
Middle Row: $65, $95 pair, $65, $65.
Bottom Row: $65 set, $75, $65, $65.

Detail of **Roses** etching.

Pink, Amber, Blue, and Green Satin #111, 12" h. Egyptian Vases. $125 each.
White Satin #20, 5.25" h. x 5.25" w. Vase. $55.
These vases date to c. 1919. Produced at Factory R, this Roses etching is different from the Roses plate etching found on Tiffin's #14180 stem line.

Rosemary.
Green #310 1/2, 6" Footed Marmalade. $35.
Pink #310 1/2, 5" Footed Marmalade. $35.
Trojan.
Green #315, 7.25" Low Foot Comport. $50.
The Rosemary and Trojan etchings were produced at Factory G c. 1930. Both etchings were used solely for tableware or serving pieces. Rosemary is a floral etching, while Trojan has a basket motif with a large ribbon tied to the handle. Rosemary is found exclusively on the #310 1/2 line.

Detail of **Rosemary** etching.

Detail of **Trojan** etching.

Brocade.
Black #15320, 10" x 5.5" h. Footed Cheese and Cracker with Cover. $275.
The Brocade etching is only found on bright black blanks. This design is identical to "Flower Garden with Butterflies" except Brocade has an etched background. "Flower Garden with Butterflies" was produced in pastel colors using different blanks than the Brocade etching. Both patterns were produced at Factory K.

Detail of **Brocade** etching.

Brocade.
Black:
#15320, 10" h. Candlesticks. $375 pair.
#15319, 10" h. Two Handled Vase. $325.

Cut #160 Design. 1927 catalog page, Factory GCS.
Top Row: $45, Cream and Sugar $35, $35, $45.
Middle Row: $35, $45 pair, $35, $35 set.
Bottom Row: $35, $30, $45, $35 set.

Cut #164 Design. 1928 catalog page, Factory GCS.
Top Row: $35, $35.
Middle Row: $35, $25, $45, $45, $25.
Bottom Row: $35, $25, $75, $25, $35.

Florice. 1927 catalog page, Factory GCS. Top Row: $35 set, Cream and Sugar $35, $35, $25. Middle Row: $25, $45 pair, Candy Box $35, $35, $45. Bottom Row: $45, $35, $35 set.

Cut #83 Design. 1928 catalog page, Factory U. The No. 167 pattern refers to the heavy thick blanks. Top Row: $25, $35 set, $15, $25. Upper Middle Row: $35, $25, $25, $35, $25. Lower Middle Row: $25, $25, $25, $25. Bottom Row: $35, $25, $25, $25, $15.

Ambassador. 1928 catalog page, Factory GCS.
Top Row: $45, $35, $45 set, $35, $35.
Upper Middle Row: $35, $45 set, $35.
Lower Middle Row: $45, $35 pair, $35, $35.
Bottom Row: $35 set, $35, $35.

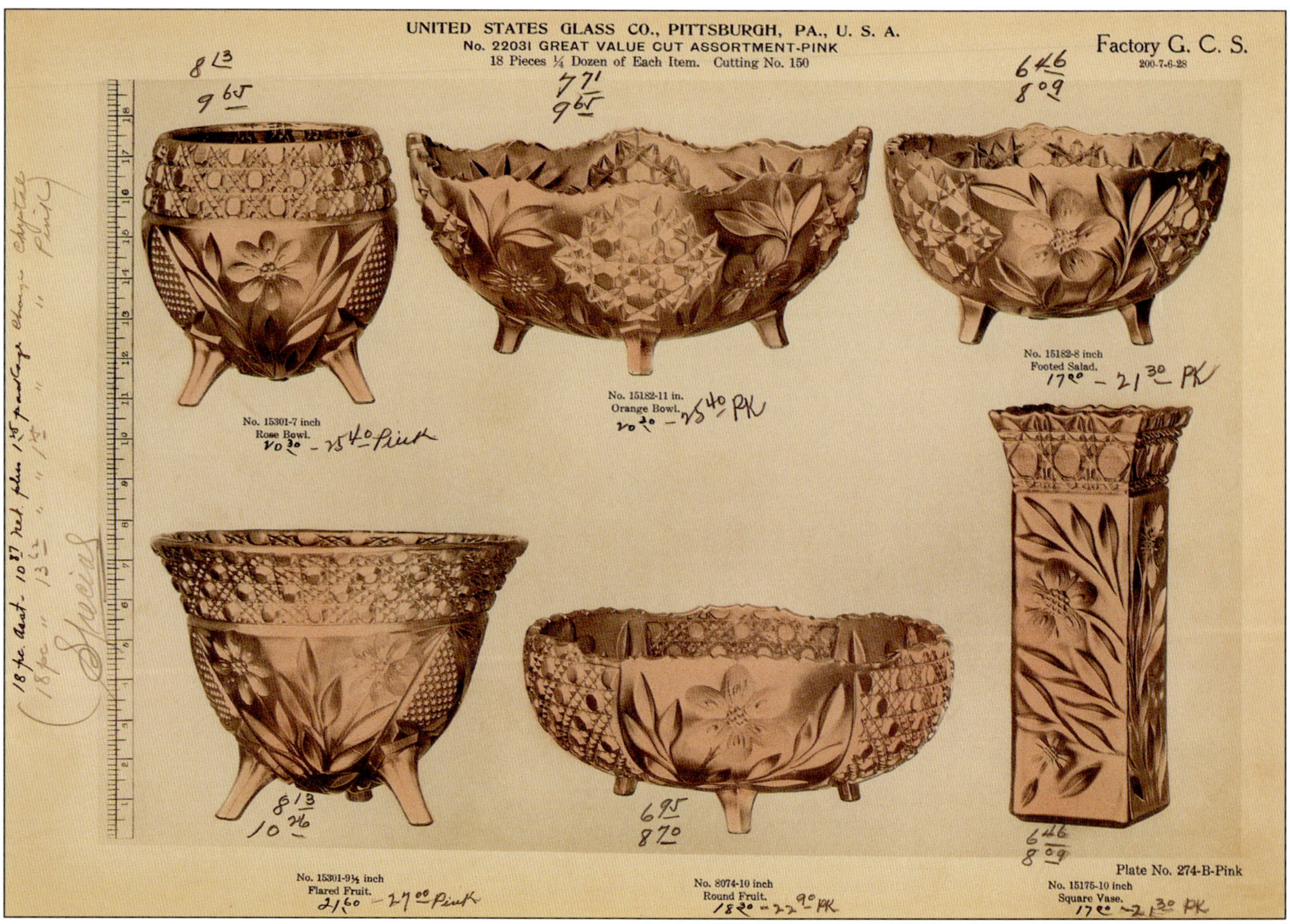

Cut #150 Design. 1928 catalog page, Factory GCS.
Top Row: $65, $65, $65.
Bottom Row: $65, $65, $75.

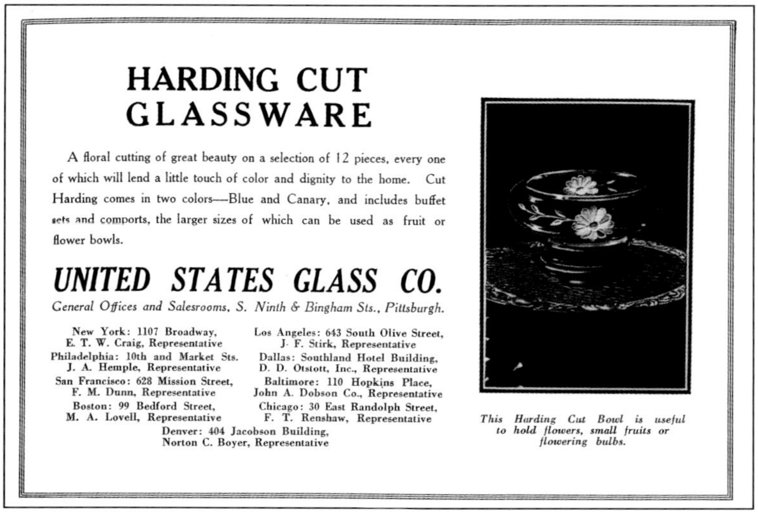

China, Glass and Lamps advertisement, October 16, 1922, **Harding** cutting.

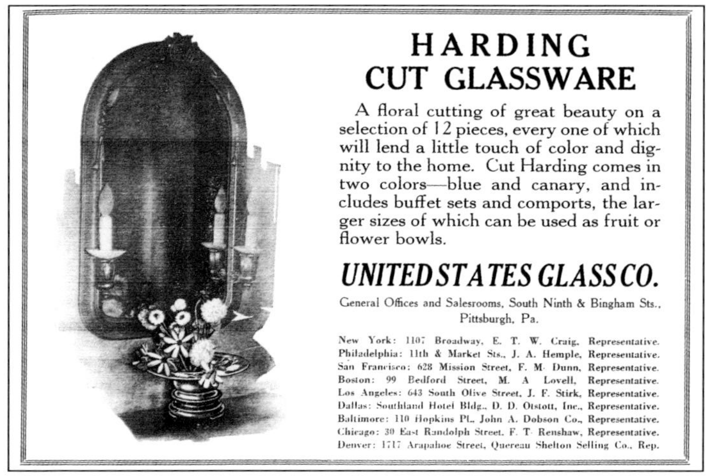

China Glass and Lamps advertisement, October 2, 1922.

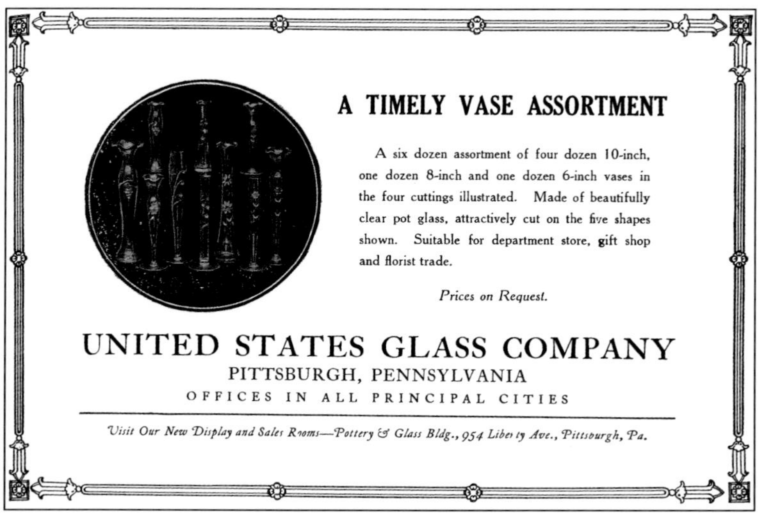

China, Glass and Lamps advertisement, June 9, 1924. These bud vases were produced at Factory R.

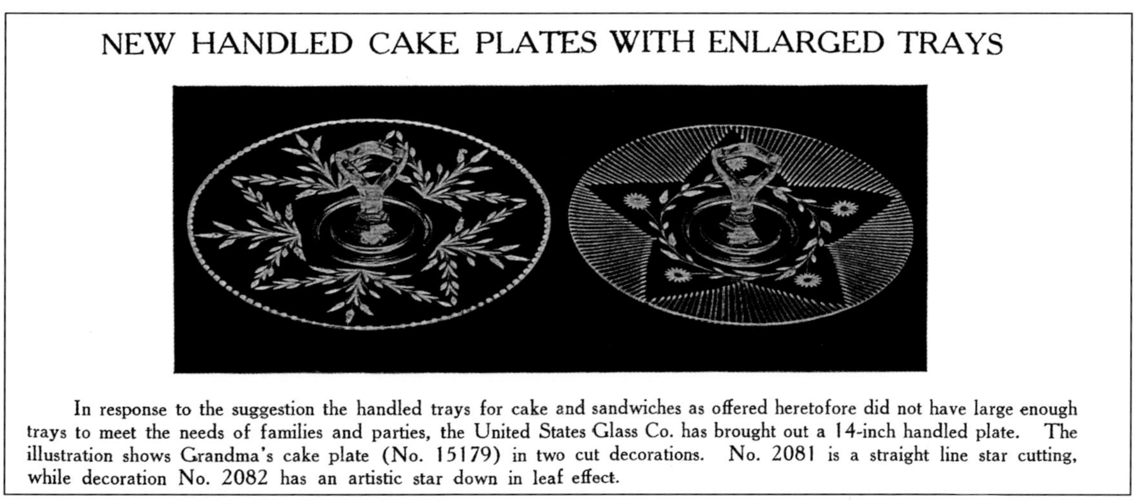

China, Glass and Lamps advertisement, July 7, 1924.

Harding.
Blue #315, 9.75" h. Candlesticks. $95 pair.
The Harding cutting consists of a daisy-like flower with leaves. It was available in twelve items in canary or blue.

Chapter 5

Lines, Patterns, and Treatments

As early as October, 1921, U. S. Glass referred to its iridized stretch glass line as Aurora.

An entry from the January 16, 1922, trade journal, *China, Glass and Lamps,* reads in part:

> By far the most striking section is that on the second floor given over to the display of new lines of colored glassware from Factory D. The new colorings and shapes include the "Cumula," the "Pomona," the "Autumn," and others.
>
> The "Cumula" comes in three color combinations: light green and white, blue and white, and pink and white. The shapes of the bowls, compotes and other articles is distinctive, while the blending of the colors, the basic color flowing into the white in an unusual manner, is above the ordinary. A striking fruit motif denotes the "Pomona" line. The colors are blue, green, purple and a combination of light tones. From the bottom the coloring deepens until near the top where it blends into a pearl shade. The border contains sprays of fruit contrasting with the body color in an attractive manner. The "Autumn" coloring is a line of lustre bowls of a near-copper shading.
>
> Several new and striking color effects have been added to the "Aurora" line which was introduced some months ago. In addition to the plain lustre there are light green and blue lustres. A touch has been given by the addition of black borders to the green and blue lustres and blue to the plain lustre. This ware comes in a fetching shape and runs the full gamut of tableware.
>
> In addition there are lines in solid green with black bases and in deep purple with black. In other new lines of blue, green, and pink lustre there will be found ice tea and water sets. No less surprising than the ware are the prices.
>
> On the flint glass floor a section has been given over to the lustre ware of Factory K, in which will be found console sets, fruit sets, plates and flower bowls in green, yellow, blue and plain lustre. In heavy wares there is lavender, coral and green colorings.

A May 29, 1922, *China, Glass and Lamps* advertisement lists a Banded Aurora decoration, consisting of canary, blue, or iridescent crystal with decorative bands of black.

The Cumula decoration was the subject of an April 24, 1922, *China, Glass and Lamps* promotional advertisement. The descriptive advertisement states that buffet sets, fruit bowls, bon bons, and various sizes of plates were available with a green cloud decoration on translucent iridescent background.

U. S. Glass also advertised its stretch glass line under the Florentine name. A September 25, 1922, *China, Glass and Lamp,* advertisement describes Florentine as opalescent glass with an iridescent sheen. The colors nile green and mandarin yellow were available with or without black bands and with plain or serrated edges.

In addition to the previously listed names, a 1923 *China, Glass and Lamps* advertisement listed Lustreline as another name for the Aurora stretch glass line. An article in *China, Glass and Lamps,* January 18, 1926, related the introduction of ruby stretch glass. Ruby is one of the most elusive colors to find in the Aurora line. A decoration that is difficult to find is Wild Rose. A 1930 inventory reveals Wild Rose is a painted decoration, found only on pink #15310 blanks.

Aurora. Blue: #151, 5" h. x 5.75" w. Vase. $45. Unidentified line number, 10" Bowl. $45. Bowl has six sets of paired optic lines and scalloped edge. #310, 9" h. Candlesticks. $95 pair.

Aurora.
Canary #151, 8" h. Lily Vase. $85.
Florentine.
Nile Green #310, 8.75" h. Candlestick. $65.
Aurora.
Crystal #315, 9.75" h. Candlestick. $55.
Canary #315, 9.75" h. Candlestick. $75.
Amber, unidentified line number, 10.5" Rolled Edge Bowl. $35.
Bowl has six sets of paired optic lines and scalloped edge.
Pink #310, 6.5" h. x 7" w. High Foot Comport, **Wild Rose** decoration. $115.
Olive green #15314, 6.75" Whipped Cream. $35.
The #15314 line is characterized by having four sets of paired optic lines in the bowls of the pieces.

Aurora.
Pink #15310, 6" h. 7" w. High Foot Comport, **Wild Rose** decoration. $115.

China, Glass and Lamps advertisement, 1923. Lusterline was another name for the stretch glass line, Aurora.

Aurora. 1928 catalog page, Factory K. U. S. Glass called its stretch glass line, Aurora. Top Row: $55 pair, $45. Upper Middle Row: $45, $35, $55 set, $45, $45. Lower Middle Row: $55, $55, $45, $55. Bottom Row: $45, $55 pair, $55 set, $45.

Florentine. Mandarin Yellow: Unidentified line number, 7" Cupped Low Foot Comport. $45. #310, 8.75" h. Candlestick. $65. Unidentified line number, 8.75" Flared Low Foot Comport. $45. Florentine was another line produced with the Aurora effect. The two comports each have six sets of paired optic lines and slightly scalloped edges.

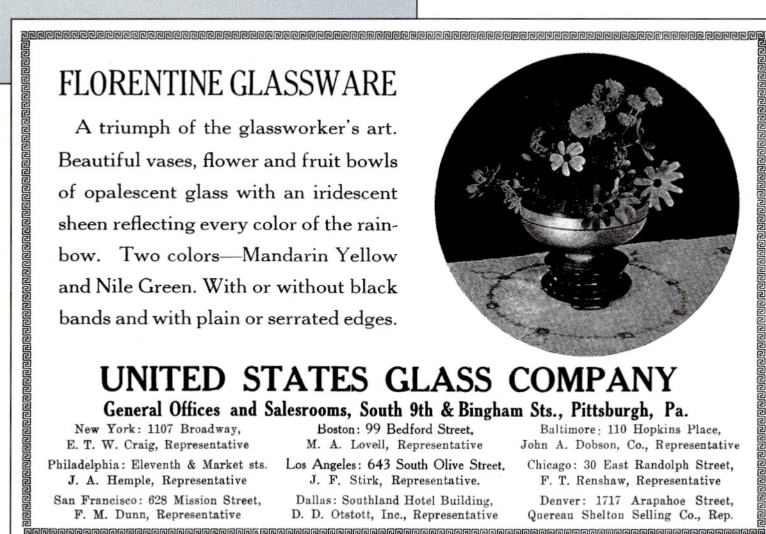

China, Glass and Lamps advertisement, September 25, 1922.

Florentine.
Nile Green, unidentified line number:
7" Flared Bowl. $45.
4.5" Sherbet. $25.
8.75" Cupped Bowl. $45.
All items have six sets of paired optic lines and a slight scallop. Note the variance in the nile green color.

#15326.
Pink:
5" Low Candleholders. $115 pair.
7.5" h. x 5" w. Comport and Cover. $115.
10" Handled Cake Plate. $65.
Whipped Cream and Ladle. $65 set.
Hazel Weatherman called the #15326 line "Flower Garden with Butterflies" in *Colored Glassware of the Depression Era 2*. This name has been accepted and used by collectors to identify this pattern. The #15326 line was produced at Factory K.

Assortment of **"Flower Garden with Butterflies" #15326:**
Amber 6" h. Vase. $75.
Green (Reflex) 10.5" h. Vase. $175.
Amber 6" h. Low Foot Puff Box and Cover. $115.
Green (Emerald) 10" Low Foot Flared Comport. $85.
Canary 6" Combination Smokers Tray. $225.
Blue 8.5" h. Candlestick. $65.

Detail of **"Flower Garden with Butterflies"** pattern.

China, Glass and Lamps advertisement, September 14, 1925. The pendant candlestick and fish bowl are seldom seen. The #15326 comport is more commonly referred to as the "Flower Garden with Butterflies" line.

Jack Frost. Undated catalog page, Factory K.
Top Row: $45 set, $65.
Middle Row: $65, $45, $85.
Bottom Row: $105, $75, $85 set.

Jack Frost.
Canary #84, 10" h. Candlestick. $55.
Canary #179, 10" Centerpiece Bowl. $75.
Pink #9574, 10.25" h. x 6" w. Basket. $85.
Crystal #9574, 10.25" h. x 6" w. Basket. $65.
Green #16261, 8.75" h. Open Work Flower Arranger Vase. $95.
Pink #18, 4.75" Low Candleholder. $35.
Green #8076, 11" Open Work Orange Bowl. $65.
Aptly named, the Jack Frost decoration has the appearance of a windowpane on a cold winter day. This decoration is only found on canary, green, pink, and crystal blanks.

Jack Frost.
Pink #8132, 6" Heart Bon Bon and Cover. $155. The cover has the Jack Frost design, the bottom has a satin finish.
Green #179, 7.5" h. Conic Candy Jar and Cover. $75.

Detail of **Jack Frost** design.

Carrara.
Pearl Blue:
#15151, 6" h. Cupped Dahlia Vase. $65.
#15151, 8" h. Cupped Dahlia Vase. $75.
#15151, 10" h. Flared Dahlia Vase. $85.
#10, 3.75" Low Candleholder. $30.
#151, 9" h. Candlesticks. $125 pair.
Carrara ware is aptly named, as carrara is a type of Italian marble. A February 13, 1922, *China, Glass, and Lamps* advertisement lists the colors as pearl gray, coral, and jade.

Look For These Patterns at the Chicago Exhibit

Visiting buyers will find a wealth of beauty in the decorated and col ored ware being shown, some of it for the first time, at the Chicago Exhibit.

Ask to be shown the Carrara ware—pearl blue, coral and jade green in solid color buffet sets. See the Aurora—plain, banded and with cumulus decorations. And the Canterbury—a beautiful glass with blue or ruby bands having fine cut effects penetrating the color. The Lincoln—in crystal, blue and canary with cut effects. The Pamono—crystal body, black footed, and color decorations on a background of clouds.

UNITED STATES GLASS COMPANY

General Offices and Salesrooms, South 9th & Bingham Sts., Pittsburgh, Pa.

New York: 1107 Broadway, E. T. W. Craig, Representative	Boston: 127 Federal Street, M. A. Lovell, Representative	Baltimore: 110 Hopkins Place, John A. Dobson, Co., Representative
Philadelphia: Eleventh & Market sts. J. A. Hemple, Representative	Los Angeles: 634 South Olive Street, J. F. Strik, Representative	Chicago: 30 East Randolph Street, F. T. Renshaw, Representative
San Francisco: 628 Mission Street, F. M. Dunn, Representative	Dallas: Southland Hotel Building, D. D. Otstott, Inc., Representative	Denver: 1717 Arapahoe Street, Quereau Shelton Selling Co., Rep.

China, Glass, and Lamps advertisement, February 6, 1922.
Note the colors are listed as pearl blue, coral, and jade green.

Carrara.
Jade Green:
#15151, 6" h. Flared Dahlia Vase. $65.
#10, 3.75" Low Candleholders. $60 pair.
#8076, 11" Open Work Orange Bowl. $75.

Carrara.
Coral:
#151, 9" h. Candlesticks. $125 pair.
#8076, 11" Open Work Orange Bowl. $75.

Carrara.
Coral:
#151, 9" h. Candlesticks. $125 pair.
#8098, 11" Orange Bowl and #9441, 5" Base. $135 set.
#15151, 10" h. Flared Dahlia Vase. $75.
#15151, 8" h. Flared Dahlia Vase. $65.
#151, 8" h. Lily Vase. $65.
The Carrara bases are considered extremely rare.

Carrara.
Coral #179, 6.5" Lily Bowl with banded decoration. $85.

Carrara.
Coral #15151, 8" h. and 6" h. Cupped Dahlia Vases. $65, $55. Note the variance of the coral color with the other items shown.

Carrara.
Coral:
#65, 9.5" h. Candlesticks. $165 pair.
#310, 9.5" Low Foot Comport. $75.
U. S. Glass marketed this style of candlestick as a Jacobean candlestick for the British market.

Carrara.
Coral #8076, 10" Open Work Orange Bowl. $125.
The rim of the bowl has been pulled up and flared out.

Carrara.
#15179, 6" Small Sweet Pea Vase. $75.
The unlisted color is an unusual purple opaque.

Brilliancy.
Green #15328:
8" h. Candlesticks. $95 pair.
7.5" Cupped Rose Bowl. $65.
Some U. S. Glass advertisements for Brilliancy refer to it as stippled glass.

Brilliancy. c. 1925 catalog page, Factory G.
Top Row: $55, $75, $85, $75.
Middle Row: $45, $35, $65, $25, $35.
Bottom Row: $35, $35, $75 pair, $55, $35, $45.

Brilliancy.
Blue #15328, 11" h. No. 1 Basket. $75.
Canary #179, 7.5" h. Conic Candy Jar with Cover. $75.
Green #15328, 12" h. No. 3 Basket. $75.
Brilliancy was produced on bright colored blanks in blue, canary, amber, and green. It has the appearance of tooled leather and was produced at Factory G.

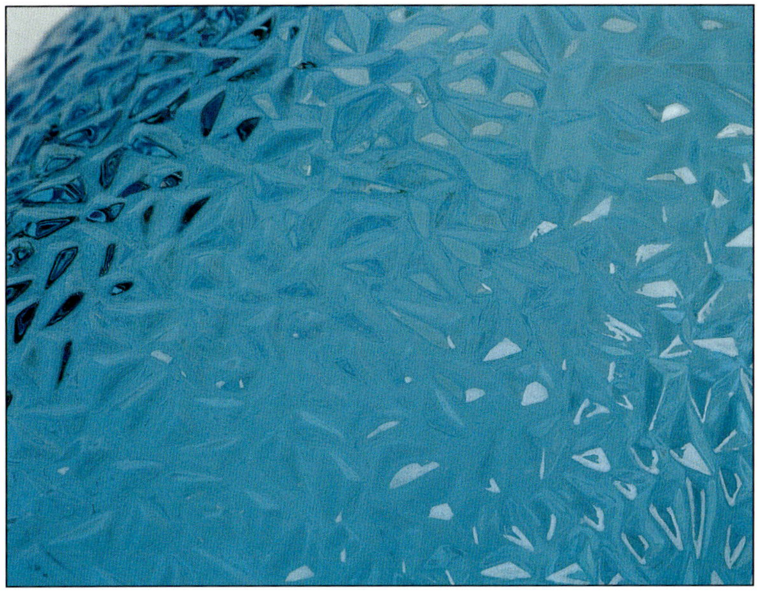

Detail of **Brilliancy** texture.

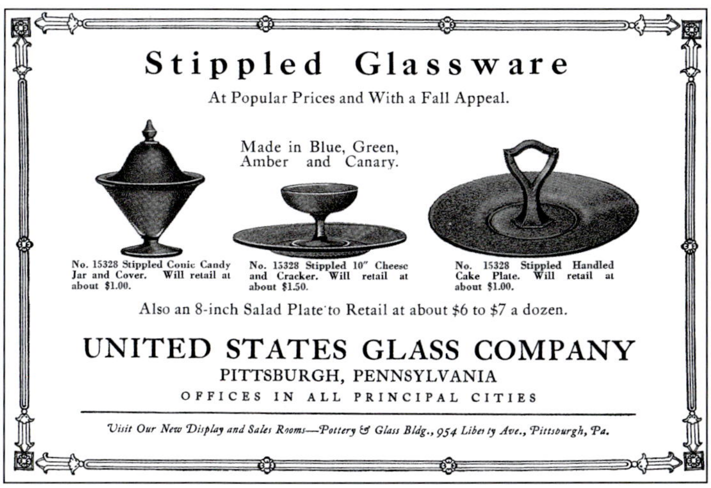

China, Glass and Lamps advertisement, July 1, 1925. These stippled glassware items are part of the Brilliancy assortment and are not shown on the catalog page.

China, Glass and Lamps advertisement, c. 1925. Additional items are from the stippled glassware Brilliancy line.

Undated catalog page, Factory K. This catalog page features seasonal colors red and green for the #15310 line. This line was heavily utilized by U. S. Glass starting in early 1922 and continuing through the 1930s. Many colors and treatments can be found, including Aurora, satin finish, painted decorations, etchings, and cuttings. Top Row: $30, $35, $55 set. Middle Row: $85 pair, $65 set. Bottom Row: $45, $35, $45 set, $55.

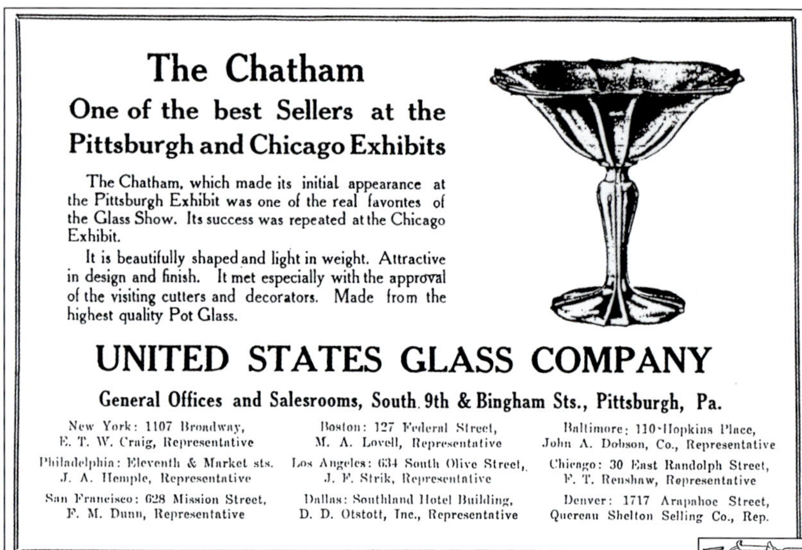

China, Glass, and Lamps advertisement, March 6, 1922, illustrating the **#15310** line as Chatham.

China, Glass and Lamps advertisement, July 6, 1925.

#15310:
Amber Satin 9" h. Candlestick. $35.
Emerald Green Satin 9" h. Candlestick. $45.
Twilite 7" Footed Mint. $30.
Red Satin 6.5" Footed Nut Bowl. $45.
Pink Satin 9" h. Flared Vase. $45.
Green Satin 4" Low Candleholder. $25.
Old Gold 10.25" h. x 6" w. Basket. $55.

UNITED STATES GLASS COMPANY, PITTSBURGH., PA., U. S. A.
No. 310½ Pattern.
Furnished in Green or Pink Glass.

Factory "K"
250-2-12-29

No. 310½-12" Sandwich Tray $11.30
No. 310½-Violet Bowl $5.80
No. 310½-Lo. Ft. Jelly $5.30
No. 310½-10" Pineapple Bowl $11.30
No. 310½-8" Bon Bon $5.80
No. 310½-6" Footed Marmalade, $5.30
No. 310½-5½" Footed Compote, $5.30
No. 310½-7" Footed Mint Wafer, $5.30
No. 310½-6" Conserve $5.80
No. 310½-7" Footed Desert $11.30
No. 310½-7" Ftd. Mint $5.30
No. 310½-9" Desert Compote $11.80
No. 310½-Footed Mayonnaise, $5.30
No. 310½-9 inch Bowl $11.30
No. 310½-12" Footed Muffin $11.80
No. 310½-10" Ftd. Cake Tray $11.30
No. 310½-9" Footed Nappy $11.30
No. 310½-10" Low Foot Fruit $11.80

Printed in U. S. A.
Plate No. 347

#310 1/2. 1929 catalog page, Factory K.
Very similar in appearance to the #310 line. Pieces in the #310 1/2 line are usually cupped in, while items from the #310 line generally flare out.
Top Row: $25, $20, $20, $25.
Upper Middle Row: $20 each.
Lower Middle Row: $25, $20, $25, $20, $25.
Bottom Row: $25 each.

#330. 1928 catalog page, Factory G.
Top Row: $20, $20, $25 set, $25, $20.
Middle Row: $30, $20, $20, $25.
Bottom Row: $35, $20, $35, $30, $35.

Spiral Optic. c. 1925 catalog page, Factory K.
Top Row: $75, $45, $10, $85, $25.
Middle Row: $45 set, $95 pair, $75 set, $35.
Bottom Row: $55 set, $35 set, $55 set.

Spiral Optic.
Amber #15331:
9" h. Candlesticks. $65 pair.
10.25" h. Basket. $55.
7" High Foot Comport. $45.
Not commonly found, spiral optic was also produced on canary and green blanks. It has also been seen in red with a satin finish. In the U. S. Glass numbering system sometimes a pattern line number will supersede a previous line number of an item. The basket shown here is commonly known as the #9574 shape. With the spiral optic decoration, the number changes to #15331. The #15326 "Flower Garden with Butterflies" line is another example where items are given different line numbers due to the decoration.

China, Glass and Lamps advertisement, October 19, 1925.

China, Glass and Lamps advertisement, c. 1926, featuring the seldom found #333 **Diamond Optic** pattern. Mulberry is another name for the amethyst color.

Chapter 6

Embossed Designs

U. S. Glass used relief molds to produce an embossed or raised appearance on glassware. The majority of the designs were floral decorations, which were often embellished with paint, to further enhance the design.

China, Glass and Lamps advertisement, c. 1924, #15318 **Rose** pattern.

Rose #15318:
Canary Satin 7.5" Bon Bon and Cover. $195.
Blue Satin 11.5" x 9" Comb and Brush Tray. $95.
Canary and Blue Cologne Bottles, satin finish. $250 each.

Rose.
Blue #15318:
8.75" Cupped Bowl, bright finish. $55.
7.5" Bon Bon, satin finish. $75.
7" h. x 7.5" w. High Foot Comport, satin finish. $95.
Produced at Factory G.
The Fenton Art Glass company has reproduced the Rose pattern using different molds and colors from U. S. Glass. Both company patterns are known as Rose.

Rose.
Opal #15318, 7.5" w. Bon Bon and Cover. $150.
Both the cover and color are considered rare.
Clusters of roses comprise the finial.

Rose.
Blue Satin #15318:
4.5" h. x 4.25" w. Large Trinket Box and Cover. $75.
3" h. x 3" w. Round Box and Cover. $55.
2.25" h. x 2.25" w. Round Box and Cover. $55.
4.5" Oval Covered Box. $65.
4" Trinket Box, minus cover. $40.

Rose.
Canary and Blue #15318, 9.5" Console Bowls, satin and opalescent finishes. $135, $125.
Bowls and comports in the Rose line typically have an exterior satin finish and a bright finish on the interior.

Rose. Green Satin #15318: 10.25" h. Candlesticks. $175 pair. 9.5" Console Bowl. $75. Green Satin is considered rare in this line.

Rose #15318: Black 6.25" h. Vase, bright finish. $75. Black Satin 6.25" h. Cologne, minus stopper. $150. Canary Satin 6.25" h. Vase. $115. Blue Satin 7.5" h. Cologne. $250. Canary Satin 4" Large Trinket Box, minus cover. $55. Canary Satin 10.25" h. Candlesticks. $225 pair.

Rose.
Blue Satin #15318:
10" Three Footed Flared Bowl. $65.
10" Handled Cake Plate. $145.
The cake plate rests on three rose buds.

Blue and Black #16264, 10" h. Vases, satin finish, floral design. $55 each. Most commonly found in black satin.

Black Satin #16271, 10.5" h. Vase, painted floral design. $65.

UNITED STATES GLASS CO., PITTSBURGH, PA., U. S. A.
No. 16256-5 in. POPPY VASE ASSORTMEMT (Satin Finish)
Furnished in Blue, Green, Rose Pink and Black colors.
Consisting of ⅔ Dozen of each color, Total 2⅔ Dozen.

Factory G
300-3-7-27

Price, Asst.

No. 16256-5 in. Poppy Vase. Green.

No. 16256-5 in. Poppy Vase. Black.

Price per Dozen

Color	Satin	Bright
Green	$8.00	$5.40
Amber	8.00	5.40
Blue	8.00	5.40
Black	8.00	5.40
Pink	8.80	6.00

Packed 2¾ Dozen to Barrel
Weight 110 lbs.

No. 16256-5 in. Poppy Vase. Pink.

No. 16256-5 in. Poppy Vase. Blue.

302

(Also furnished in Bright Colored Glass in Green, Black, Pink, Blue and Amber Colors.)

1927 catalog page, Factory G.
Top Row: $55, $45.
Bottom Row: $75, $85.

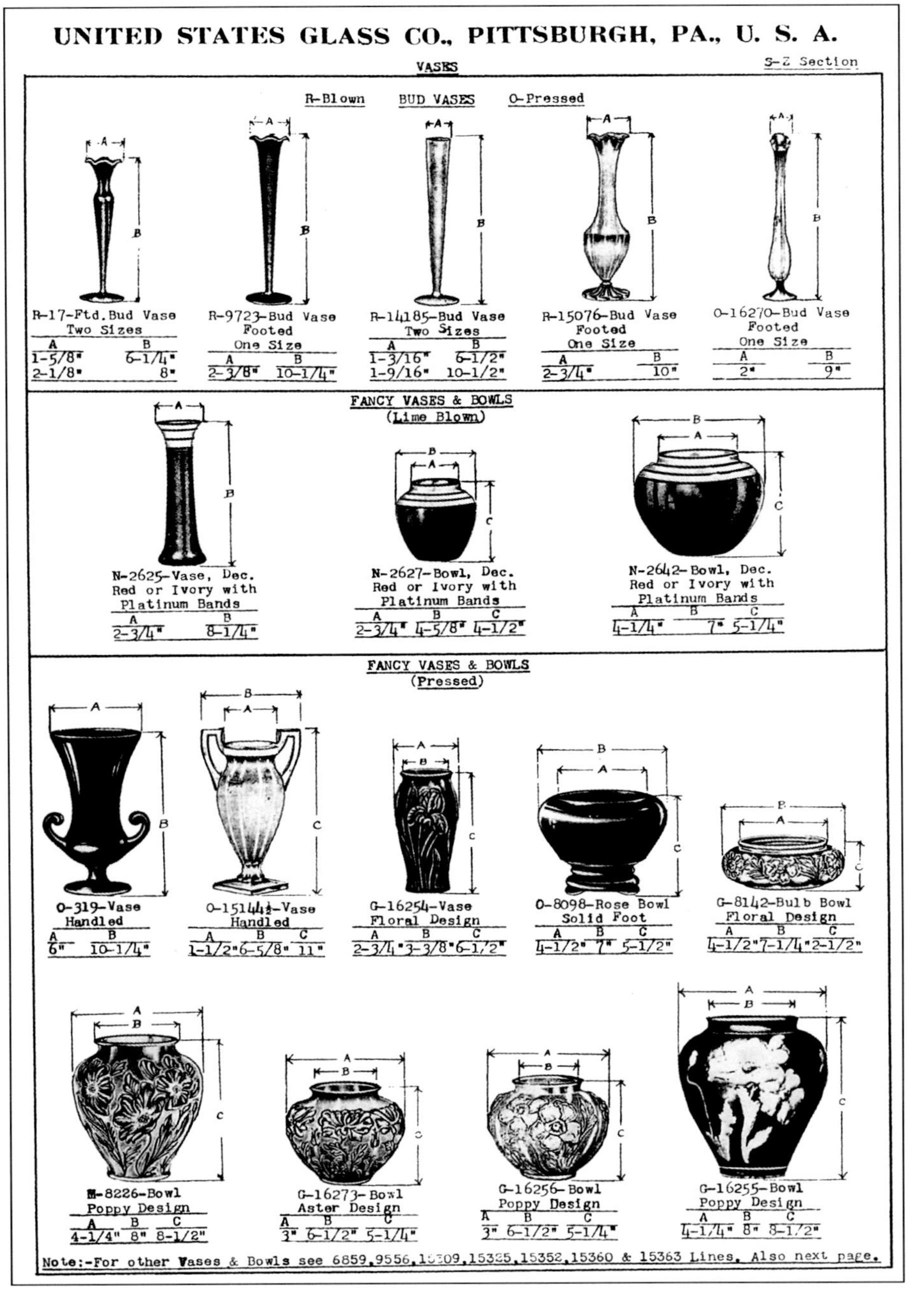
UNITED STATES GLASS CO., PITTSBURGH, PA., U. S. A.

S-Z Section

VASES

R-Blown BUD VASES O-Pressed

R-17-Ftd. Bud Vase
Two Sizes

A	B
1-5/8"	6-1/4"
2-1/8"	8"

R-9723-Bud Vase
Footed
One Size

A	B
2-3/8"	10-1/4"

R-14185-Bud Vase
Two Sizes

A	B
1-3/16"	6-1/2"
1-9/16"	10-1/2"

R-15076-Bud Vase
Footed
One Size

A	B
2-3/4"	10"

O-16270-Bud Vase
Footed
One Size

A	B
2"	9"

FANCY VASES & BOWLS
(Lime Blown)

N-2625-Vase, Dec.
Red or Ivory with
Platinum Bands

A	B
2-3/4"	8-1/4"

N-2627-Bowl, Dec.
Red or Ivory with
Platinum Bands

A	B	C
2-3/4"	4-5/8"	4-1/2"

N-2642-Bowl, Dec.
Red or Ivory with
Platinum Bands

A	B	C
4-1/4"	7"	5-1/4"

FANCY VASES & BOWLS
(Pressed)

O-319-Vase
Handled

A	B
6"	10-1/4"

O-15144½-Vase
Handled

A	B	C
1-1/2"	6-5/8"	11"

G-16254-Vase
Floral Design

A	B	C
2-3/4"	3-3/8"	6-1/2"

O-8098-Rose Bowl
Solid Foot

A	B	C
4-1/2"	7"	5-1/2"

G-8142-Bulb Bowl
Floral Design

A	B	C
4-1/2"	7-1/4"	2-1/2"

M-8226-Bowl
Poppy Design

A	B	C
4-1/4"	8"	8-1/2"

G-16273-Bowl
Aster Design

A	B	C
3"	6-1/2"	5-1/4"

G-16256-Bowl
Poppy Design

A	B	C
3"	6-1/2"	5-1/4"

G-16255-Bowl
Poppy Design

A	B	C
4-1/4"	8"	8-1/2"

Note:-For other Vases & Bowls see 6859, 9556, 15309, 15325, 15352, 15360 & 15363 Lines. Also next page.

1937 catalog page.
Note the difference in design of the two large poppy bowls at the bottom of the page.

China, Glass and Lamps advertisement, 1925.

#16255, 8.5" h. x 8" w. Poppy Vases:
Black Satin. $65.
White Satin. $75. Poppies on the vase have a bright finish.
Green Satin. $105.
Pink Satin. $105.
The #16255 vases were produced at Factory G, and can also be found in amber, canary, and blue with a bright or satin finish. Very common in black satin.

White Satin #8226, 8.5" h. x 8" w. Poppy Vase. $35.
The #8226 is the same size, but differs in design from the #16255 poppy vase. The decoration on the #8226 vase consists of three embossed poppy flowers with a long serrated leaf along the length of the vase. The #16255 vase has two embossed poppy flowers. The #8226 vase was produced in the mid 1930s in crystal and opal. It is usually found with a white satin finish. The crystal vases were also cold painted on the interior with red, green, brown, or black paint.
The blue satin vase is a reproduction dating from the 1980s. It is the same design as the #8226 vase; however, the neck of the vase has been cut down. The reproduction vase carried a paper label which read in part "Cambridge Glass, Hand Blown U. S. A." It was available in blue or pink with a satin finish. This vase was not a product of the well-known Cambridge Glass Company of Cambridge, Ohio.

#16256, 5" h. x 6" w. Poppy Vases:
Pink Satin. $75.
Blue Satin. $85.
Black Satin. $45.
Canary Satin. $85.
Ruby Satin, coralene decoration. $275.
Green Satin. $55.
Also found in amber and white satin. The poppy vases were available with a bright finish and were produced at Factory G. The #16256 poppy vase was in production for over ten years and is readily available today.

Detail of #16256 Poppy Vase.

Green, Pink, and Blue #16256, 6" w. x 6.5" h. Bath Salt Jars, satin finish. $235 each.
These were shown in a 1930 advertisement. U. S. Glass combined the #16256 poppy vase and a cover from the #15318 Rose line to create the bath salt jar. It can be found in the other poppy vase colors as well.

Black Satin #16273, 5" h. x 6" w. Aster Bowl or Vase. $55.
Produced at Factory G, the aster vase can also be found in blue, green, and canary.

Canary Satin:
#310, 7" Open Work Bon Bon. $75.
#8142, 7" Powder Box with Cover. $215.
Most commonly found in black, the powder box was also produced in pink, green, and blue. U. S. Glass also marketed the #8142 powder box under other names, e.g. bon bon with cover, squat bowl, bulb bowl, and lilique bowl.

$6.00 Bright
8.00 Satin

UNITED STATES GLASS CO., PITTSBURGH, PA., U. S. A.
No. 8142—LILIQUE BOWLS.
Furnished in Black, Green and Pink, Satin Finish, Plain and Decorated.

16.00

Factory "G & N"
200-11-21-27

G—8142—Lilique Bowl, Satin Finish, Black.
Also furnished in Bright.

N—8142—Lilique Bowl, Satin Finish, Green Floral Decoration.

G—8142—Lilique Bowl, Satin Finish, Pink.
Also furnished in Bright.

N—8142—Lilique Bowl, Satin Finish, Pink Floral Decoration.

G—8142—Lilique Bowl, Satin Finish, Green.
Also furnished in Bright.

N—8142—Lilique Bowl, Satin Finish, Black Floral Decoration.

333

Lilique Bowls. 1927 catalog page. The bowls were produced at Factory G, and decorated at Factory N.
Top Row: $45, $75.
Middle Row: $45, $75.
Bottom Row: $45, $75.

#16254, 6" h. Iris Vases with satin finish:
Black $65.
Green $85.
Canary $95.
Pink $85.
White $95.
The iris vases, produced at Factory G, were also made in blue and amber.

Smoke #16254, 6" h. Iris Vase, satin finish. $35.
Pink #16254, 6" h. Iris Vase, satin finish, crimped rim. $45.
The Tiffin Glass Company, formerly Factory R, reproduced the iris vases in the 1970s. The vases were lighter in weight and sometimes came with a crimped rim. They were produced in smoke, black, pink, and crystal, with a bright or satin finish.

Black Satin #9298, 6" Stag Ash Tray. $55.
The design consists of a moose trampling a wolf. Available only in black.

Black Satin #9298, 6" Ash Tray. $55. The design consists of a well-detailed building and block lettering that reads "1902-1928 Carnegie National Bank." This ash tray was private mold work and was not available to the general public. Other designs on the #9298 ash tray have been seen.

Blue:
#8130, 5" Oval Bulb Box with stippled panels. $35.
#8131, 7.5" Oblong Bulb Box with mitered corners. $45.
#8127, 9.5" Oblong Bulb Box, satin finish. $115.
The #8130 and #8131 bulb boxes were also produced in amber and green, and are more difficult to find than the #8127 bulb box.

Blue Satin:
Unidentified line number, 10" Dresser Tray, gold trim. $85.
#8127, 9.5" x 4" x 4" Oblong Bulb Box with mitered corners. $115.
Both items have a design of ladies frolicking to music of the harp and lute. Also available in black, green (emerald and reflex), white, pink, canary, and amber, with a bright or satin finish.

China, Glass and Lamps advertisement, c. 1926.

China, Glass and Lamps advertisement, April 20, 1925. This ad is one of the few known references to the #15314 line.

China, Glass and Lamps advertisement, October 13, 1924.

Canary Satin #16263, 6" h. x 5" w. Wall Vase. $95. The face of the wall vase has an embossed exotic flower on a pseudo-crackled texture. This vase is usually found in black with a bright finish, but was also produced in blue and green with a satin finish.

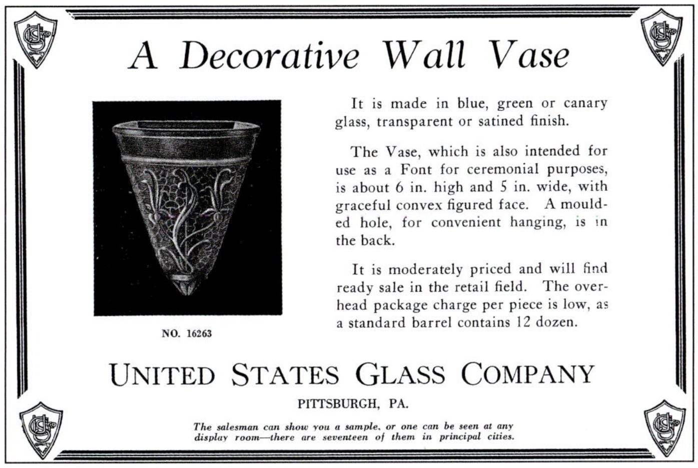

China, Glass and Lamps advertisement, January 24, 1927.

Amethyst:
#8220, 7" Two-light Candleholders. $215 pair.
#8220-3, 13" Centerpiece Bowl. $75.
Colors produced at Factory G in the mid 1930s were amethyst, green, black, and crystal.

Detail of panel design on the candleholders and centerpiece bowl.

Green:
#8220, 7" Two-light Candleholders. $215 pair.
#8220-3, 13" Centerpiece Bowl. $75.

Green #8220, 7" Three-light Candleholder. $115.
Amethyst Satin #8220, 12.5" h. x 13" w. Basket. $125.
Black Satin #8220, 7" Three-light Candleholder. $115.
Three styles of centerpiece bowls and a torte plate were also produced in the #8220 line. This line is most commonly found in crystal or black.

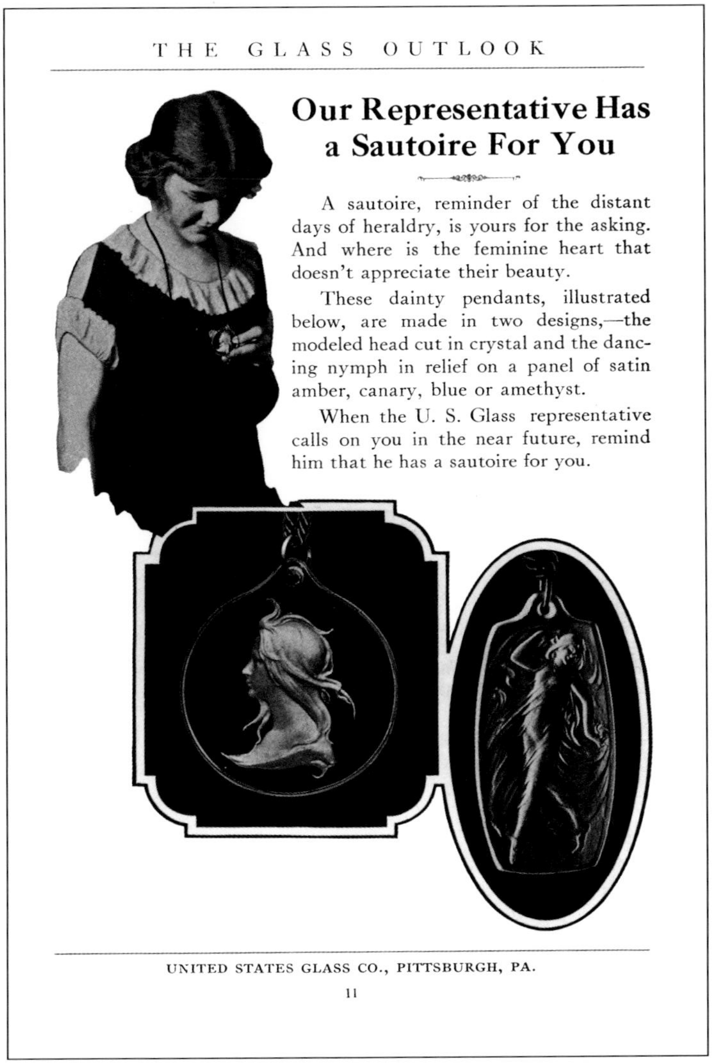

The Glass Outlook, February 1924.
The Glass Outlook was an in-house publication by U. S. Glass that promoted their newest and most popular products. The pamphlet was issued monthly in 1924, with possible further publication in 1925.

China, Glass and Lamps advertisement, c. 1927. The ash trays were produced with a bright or satin finish.

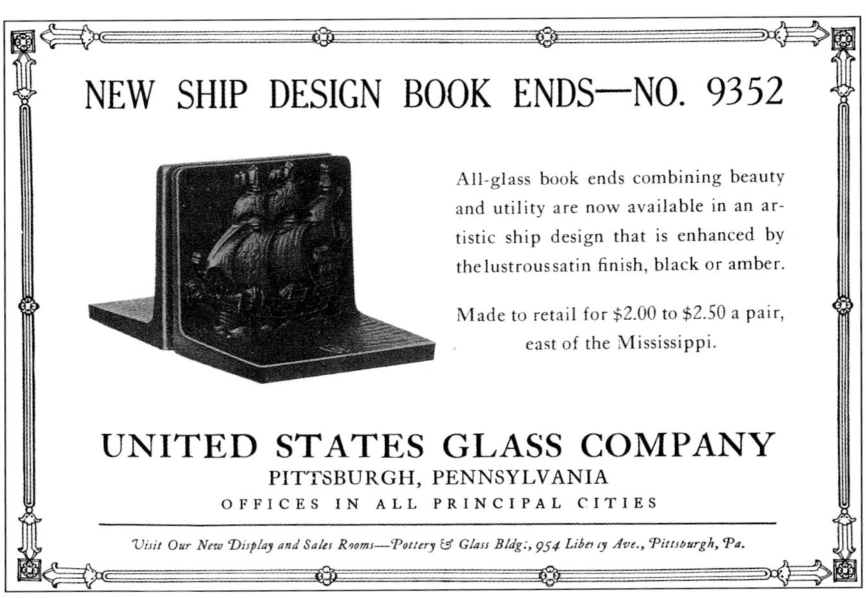

China, Glass and Lamps advertisement, October 26, 1925.

Chapter 7

Decorations by Other Companies

Design #51, "Drapes."
Black Satin:
#319, 10" h. Candlesticks. $115 pair.
#179, 11" Orange Bowl. $75.
#9574, 10.25" x 6" w. Basket. $85.
The Wheeling Decorating Company of Wheeling, West Virginia, decorated these items and designated the decoration as Design #51. Collectors have since named it "Drapes." The "Drapes" design has only been seen on black satin blanks from U. S. Glass; however, Wheeling used the "Drapes" decoration on items from several other glass companies.

Design #51, "Drapes."
Black Satin:
#151, 9" h. Candlesticks. $115 pair.
#179, 7" Candy Box with Cover and #9442, 3.5" Base. $115 set.
Decorated by the Wheeling Decorating Company of Wheeling, West Virginia.

Detail of **"Drapes"** decoration by the Wheeling Decorating Company.

Black Satin:
#151, 9" h. Candlesticks. $125 pair.
#179, 9" Low Foot Comport. $75.
This design appeared in a c. late 1920s catalog of Consolidated Lamp and Glass Company using several U. S. Glass black satin blanks. The design consists of a multi-color bird perched on a stem of white flowers. This enameled decoration is generally found in fine condition.

Black Satin:
#151, 8.5" h. Small Lily Vase, $75.
#15151, 8" h. Flared Dahlia Vase, $75.

Detail of the multi-color bird decoration.

Blue Satin #320, 9" h. Wall Vase with silver overlay decoration by Rockwell Silver Company. $215. The vases can also be found in jasper, royal blue, canary, black, pink, amber, amethyst, and ruby. This style of wall vase is the most common of the U. S. Glass wall vases. Most of the silver overlay designs found on U. S. Glass blanks were decorated by the Rockwell Silver Company of Meriden, Connecticut. Rockwell was not a glass manufacturer, but purchased blanks from many glass companies to decorate. Occasionally, the acid stamp of the Rockwell shield can be faintly seen on the bases of items.

Line drawing of the acid stamp Rockwell Silver Company logo found on the bases of decorated items. This acid stamp, one-quarter inch in height, is shaped like a shield. The design includes three boars heads at the top of the shield, with the wording "Rockwell Silver Company, since 1907." Rockwell used this style of acid stamp through 1968. The company went out of business in 1980. More information on Rockwell can be found in an article written by Roserita Ziegler for *Glass Review,* April 1981.

Blue Satin:
#151, 7" h. Flared Footed Vase. $115.
#179, 10" h. Candy Jar with Cover. $155.
#74, 10" h. Candlesticks. $225 pair.
All items have the identical silver overlay design.

Blue Satin:
#179, 10" Handled Cake Plate. $115.
#15319, 6" h. Two Handled Vase. $145.
#151, 10" h. Two Handled Vase. $165.
All items are decorated with the same silver overlay design. This design is most frequently found on blue satin blanks.

Black Satin #15151, 10" h. and 8" h. Cupped Dahlia Vases with "thistle" silver overlay design by Rockwell Silver Company. $195, $175.
Green Satin #20, 6" Globe Vase, wide optic, with "thistle" silver overlay design by Rockwell Silver Company. $155.

Black Satin #15151:
8" h. Cupped Dahlia Vase with "iris" silver overlay design. $195.
6" h. Cupped Dahlia Vase with silver overlay design and enameled tropical bird, decorated by Rockwell Silver Company. $195.

Black Satin #15151, 6" h. Cupped Dahlia Vase with silver overlay decoration. $155.
Black #15151, 8" h. Flared Dahlia Vase with all-over floral silver overlay decoration. $175.

Black Satin:
#82, 8.5" h. Candlesticks. $225 pair.
#15179, 8.5" Flower Bowl with #9440, 6" Base. $165 set.
The silver overlay decoration has geese flying over evergreen trees as its motif. Decorated by Rockwell Silver Company.

Black Satin #16258, 9" h. Wall Vase with silver overlay decoration by Rockwell Silver Company. $225.
The wall vases were produced at Factory G in amber, jasper, royal blue, amethyst, blue, and canary. Collectors sometimes refer to this wall vase as the half-round style.

Green Satin #15151:
8" h. Cupped Dahlia Vase. $155.
10" h. Flared Dahlia Vase. $165.
Each vase is decorated with a different style of ship.

Green Satin #14185, 10.25" h. Bud Vase, painted decoration by Ransburg. $55.
The Harper J. Ransburg Company was founded in 1911, in Indianapolis, Indiana. The company was known for its patented electrostatic painting process that was used on glass, stoneware, metal, and plastic products. Illinois Tool Works purchased Ransburg in 1989.

Detail of Ransburg label, which reads "Ransburg, Glass of Class, Indianapolis."

Detail of McCourt Studios label, which reads "Peacock Products, McCourt, Studios, Minneapolis."

Black Satin #16264, 10" h. Vase with floral design and coralene decoration. $250.
Occasionally items with coralene decoration can be found with the original label of the decorator, "Peacock Products, McCourt Studios, Minneapolis." Most coralene decorations are found on items with an embossed design such as the poppy, iris, and floral vases. The embossed design is painted, and very fine glass beads are applied to the paint before firing. The decoration is enhanced under ultraviolet lighting. Most coralene today is found in less than perfect condition, as the glass beading tends to fall off readily.

Black Satin:
#320, 9" h. Wall Vase. $175.
#16254, 6" h. Iris Vase. $135.
#97, 4.5" Low Poppy Candleholders. $175 pair.
These are examples of coralene decoration by McCourt Studios of Minneapolis, Minnesota. Commonly found on black, coralene can also be found on pink, canary, red, green, blue, and ruby satin blanks.

Black Satin:
#16256, 5" Poppy Bowl or Vase. $115.
#16254, 6" h. Iris Vase. $135.
Both items have coralene decoration on the embossed portions of the vases.

Black Satin #8142, 7" Powder Box with Cover, coralene decoration. $235.

Black Satin #15319, 6.25" h. Two Handled Vase, coralene decoration. $65. The same style of vase was also made in a 10" size.

Chapter 8

Unidentified Decorations

At this time, the decorations on these U. S. Glass blanks are undocumented. The designs may have been painted by U. S. Glass employees, private individuals, or the blanks may have been purchased and decorated by other companies.

"Mefford" Black Satin:
#15151, 6" h. Cupped Dahlia Vase. $45.
#15151, 8" h. Cupped Dahlia Vase. $55.
#10, 3.75" Low Candleholder. $30.
#66, 7.5" h. Candlestick. $40.
#15319, 10" h. Candlestick. $40.
Unidentified line number, 8.25" h. Candlestick. $40.
It is not known whether U. S. Glass decorated this design. Hazel Weatherman named the pattern "Mefford" in her book, *Glassware of the Depression Era 2*. The "Mefford" design has only been seen on U. S. Glass black satin blanks.

Black Satin:
#179, 7" Candy Box with Cover. $85.
#10, 3.75" Low Candleholder. $30.
#151, 7" Flower Bowl. $35.
#9574, 10.25" h. x 6" w. Basket. $75.
All items have gold-painted flowers and vines entwining the piece. Only found on black satin blanks.

Detail of gold flower design.

Black Satin:
#151, 11" h. Large Lily Vase with **Decoration #51, "Drapes",** by the Wheeling Decorating Company of Wheeling, West Virginia. $85.
#151, 8.5" h. Small Lily Vase, painted pine cone decoration. $55. Note the sizes of the two lily vases. The large lily vase is more difficult to find.

Detail of pine cone decoration.

Black Satin:
#319, 8.5" Oval Candy Box. $85.
#10, 3.75" Low Candleholders. $65 pair.
#9574, 10.25" h. x 6" w. Basket. $85.
#179, 7.5" Conic Candy Jar and Cover. $85.
This design is comprised of a clipper ship decoration painted in silver and outlined in gold. Only found on black satin blanks.

Detail of clipper ship design.

Canary Satin:
#319, 7.5" High Foot Comport. $45.
#151, 6.5" Whipped Cream. $35.
Both items have a hand-painted orange oriental poppy flower nestled between two leaves.

Detail of oriental poppy flower decoration.

Pink Satin #319, 7.5" High Foot Comport, painted iris decoration. $65.

Detail of iris decoration.

Black Satin:
#319, 8.5" Oval Candy Box and Cover. $85.
#10, 3.75" Low Candleholders. $75 pair.
#151, 10.5" Garden Bowl. $65.
#15151, 8" h. Cupped Dahlia Vase. $85.
The decoration has enameled orange stylized flowers with green leaves and stems on black satin blanks. Usually found in very good condition.

Detail of decoration.

Blue Satin #151, 8" h. Lily Vase, enameled hollyhock decoration. $55.

Detail of hollyhock decoration.

Pink Satin:
#330, 6.5" High Foot Comport. $55.
#10, 3.75" Low Candleholders. $55 pair.
#179, 7" Nasturtium Bowl. $45.
All pieces have the identical unknown enamel decoration.

Detail of enameled decoration.

Black Satin #15151:
6" h. Flared Dahlia Vase, gold daffodil decoration. $65.
8" h. Flared Dahlia Vase, gold jack-in-the-pulpit decoration. $65.

Green Satin:
#10, 3.75" Low Candleholders. $55 pair.
#330, 6" Low Foot Flared Comport. $45.
The decoration consists of pink and yellow enameled flowers with a gold band on rim and foot.

Detail of enameled decoration.

Black Satin #15151, 10" h. Cupped Dahlia Vase, painted floral decoration. $85.

Black Satin:
#9723, 10" h. Crimped Vase. $55.
#10, 3.75" Low Candleholder. $35.
#151, 8.5" h. Small Lily Vase. $65.
This unknown cattail decoration has also been seen on a Cambridge Glass Company blank.

Detail of cattail design.

Blue Satin:
#15151, 6" h. Cupped Dahlia Vases. $55 each.
#179, 7.5" h. Conic Candy Jar and Cover. $65.
The decoration consists of dot-painted flowers with black leaves. The rim and base are trimmed with white gold. Also produced on canary satin blanks.

Detail of decoration.

Black Satin #9574, 10.25" h. x 6" w. Basket, dot-painted flowers. $65. Blue Satin #179, 7" Nasturtium Bowl, dot-painted flowers. $45.

Detail of dot-painted flowers on basket.

Detail of dot-painted flowers on nasturtium bowl.

Chapter 9

Figurals

UNITED STATES GLASS CO., Factory "K" PITTSBURGH, PA.
MISCELLANEOUS COLORED WARE.
K

(†) 9448. Cat (†) 9446. Cat (†) 9445. Cat (†) 15151. Bon Bon and Cover (*) 15319. 8 in. Candlesticks (†) 69. Frog (†) 72. Frog (*) 15319. 10 in. Hi. Foot Comport

(†) 9298. Stag Ash Tray (‡) 9285. Ash Tray (*) 82. 8½ in. Candlestick (*) 15315. 10 in. Low Foot Comport (*) 82. 8½ in Candlestick (†) 9306. 6 in. Cigarette Box and Cover (†) 9305 4½ in. Cigarette Box and Cover

(‡) 15179. 10 in. Footed Comport, Flared (‡) No. 10. Candlestick. (‡) 8076. 11 in. Open Work Orange Bowl and Base (‡) No. 10. Candlestick (‡) 8076. 10 in. Open Work Berry Bowl and Base

191

— LEGEND —
(†) Black Satin. (‡) Bright Black and Black Satin. (*) Bright Red, Bright Green, Blue, Canary, Green, Red and Black Satin.

Miscellaneous Colored Ware. Undated catalog page, Factory K. Note the two sizes of cigarette boxes. Top Row: $165, $125, $325, $45, $65 pair, $110, $110, $55. Middle Row: $55, $35, $65 pair, $55, $55, $45. Bottom Row: $35, $40 pair, $75 set, $75 set.

Crystal with brown paint #9445, 5.75" h. Cat. $325. Black Satin #9446, 5.25" h. Grotesque Cat. $175. Black Satin #9448, 10.75" h. Cat. $225. The #9445 cat is the most elusive cat and is usually found in black satin. U. S. Glass also produced the #9448 cat in opal, and a rare opal and black combination. The Fenton Art Glass Company has reproduced both the #9446 and the #9448 cats in numerous colors.

Opal #9448, 11" Large Cat. $300.
Rare in opal. Introduced in 1923.

Old Gold #9213, 3.5" Dog Ash Tray. $45.
Also marketed as a pin tray. Black, pink, and green were the other production colors.

Black Satin:
#69, 5.75" h. Frog Candlestick. $125.
#72, 5.75" h. Frog Candlestick. $125.
Produced only in black, occasionally with a bright finish or painted decoration.

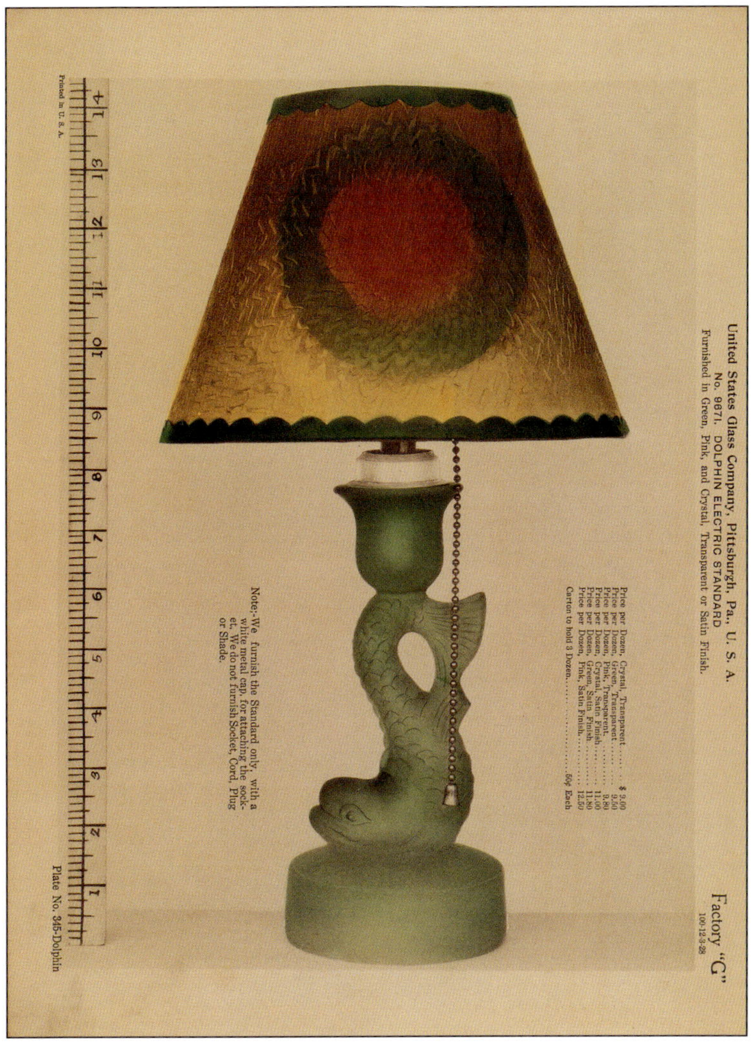

United States Glass Company, Pittsburgh, Pa., U. S. A.
No. 9671. DOLPHIN ELECTRIC STANDARD
Furnished in Green, Pink, and Crystal, Transparent or Satin Finish.

Factory "G"
100-12-3-28

Price per Dozen, Crystal, Transparent .... $ 9.00
Price per Dozen, Green, Transparent 9.50
Price per Dozen, Pink, Transparent 9.80
Price per Dozen, Crystal, Satin Finish 11.00
Price per Dozen, Green, Satin Finish 11.80
Price per Dozen, Pink, Satin Finish 12.50
Carton to hold 3 Dozen .... 60¢ Each

Note:-We furnish the Standard only, with a white metal cap, for attaching the socket. We do not furnish Socket, Cord, Plug or Shade.

Printed in U. S. A.

Plate No. 345-Dolphin

1928 catalog page, Factory G.
#9671 Dolphin Electric Standard. $195.

Green, Blue, and Pink #9671, 8" h. Dolphin Candlesticks. $65, $85, $65.
Pink and Green #9671, 4.25" h. Dolphin Candlesticks. $35, $45.
The Dolphin candlesticks are scarce with the satin finish. Also known in black and crystal. The far right candlestick has a collar on the candle cup, which was used for conversion to an electrical lamp.

Canary:
#8111, 12" w. x 7" h. Fish Bowl. $195.
Unidentified line number, 7" w. x 4" h. Dolphin Fish Globe Base. $225.
The base accommodates a fish globe with a 4.75" base.
Green #9730, 8" h. Fish Bowl with wire optic. $85.
Also made in 7" and 11" sizes.
Blue #20122, 11.5" w. x 7" h. Fish Bowl. $185.
Black, unidentified line number, 7" w. x 4" h. Dolphin Fish Globe Base. $135.
The fish globes and dolphin bases were produced in amber, blue, canary, and green. The globes were also marketed as confection jars. Some bases can be found with a satin finish. With the exception of black, dolphin bases are considered rare.

Fish Globes. Undated catalog page, Factories B, G, and U. The fish globes were produced with a bright finish, and the bases with a satin or bright finish.
Top Row: $125 set, $165 set, $95.
Bottom Row: $115 set, $325 set, $125 set, $275 set.

Fish Globes, Seed Cups and Bird Baths. Undated catalog page, Factories B, G, N, O, and R.
Top Row: $165, $125 set, $10, $135 set, $10, $125, $10.
Middle Row: $10 each.
Bottom Row: $115, $95, $85, $95.

Confection Jars. 1929 catalog page.
In addition to crystal, many of these jars were available in green or amber.

China, Glass and Lamps advertisement, January 4, 1926, showing another style of fish bowl.

Green and Pink #9313, 6.75" h. **Dancing Girl** Colognes, satin finish. $275 each.
Green Satin #9313, 6" h. Puff Box. $165.
The side panel of the cologne depicts a scantily clad woman holding a flower above her head. The identical design is also found on the #16265 torchiere lamps. The Dancing Girl dresser set was also produced in blue and white.

White, Green, and Blue #9313, 6" h. **Dancing Girl** Puff Boxes, satin finish. $115, $165, $175.
An unknown maker has reproduced the Dancing Girl puff boxes. The reproductions are called "Curtsy" by collectors, and can be found in pink, green, or blue satin, and jadeite. The reproduction is usually marked "Toussant" on the base; the Dancing Girl is unmarked. Another difference between the two puff boxes is the "Curtsy" head is more upright than the Dancing Girl head. Also, the top edge of the "Curtsy" puff box is smooth, while the top edge of the Dancing Girl puff box has a rope trim. For more information on these two styles of puff boxes, see *Bedroom and Bathroom Glassware of the Depression Years* by Margaret and Kenn Whitmyer.
Very recent reproductions, also of unknown origin, have been seen in yellow and amethyst with a bright finish.

Canary and Green, unidentified line number, 9.25" h. vases, satin finish, embossed "nymph" design. $275, $225.
The identical "nymph" design is found on the side panels of the Dancing Girl cologne. The vases are also known in black, white, blue, and pink with satin finishes.
White Satin #16265, 13.5" h. Torchiere Lamp, with black glass top and metal base. $325.
Some lamps were produced with a glass top and a satin finish base. Lamps and vases were produced in the same colors, with the exception of black. Vases were drilled to form the body of the lamp.

Green Satin, unidentified line number, 9.25" h. vase. $225. The 8.75" cobalt blue vase is a reproduction by Sarsaparilla Designs Limited from New Jersey. The reproductions date from the middle 1980s and were also made in crystal, pink and green with satin finishes. The U. S. Glass vase has a flat base, whereas the reproduction vase rests on four short feet. The reproduction vases were fitted with a metal top to form a lamp. The vases retailed for $45.00 and the lamps for $100.00.

1991 catalog page from Sarsaparilla Designs Ltd. Sarsaparilla specialized in Art Deco reproductions boasting that many of their offerings were reissued from the original molds. The #16265 torchiere lamp is shown reproduced in pink, crystal, green, and cobalt blue. The lamp was also offered without the metal top for use as a vase.

Chapter 10

Vanity Items

Pink Satin #331 **Milady** Dresser Set:
5.5" h. Colognes. $75 each.
3.5" h. Puff Box. $45.
10" Dresser Tray. $35.
Produced at Factory K, the dresser sets were also available in black, blue, green (emerald and reflex), amber, canary, crystal, and ivory.

Ivory #331:
5.5" h. **Milady** Colognes, gold trim. $85 each.
3.5" **Milady** Puff Box, gold trim. $65.
Items in this opaque color are scarce.

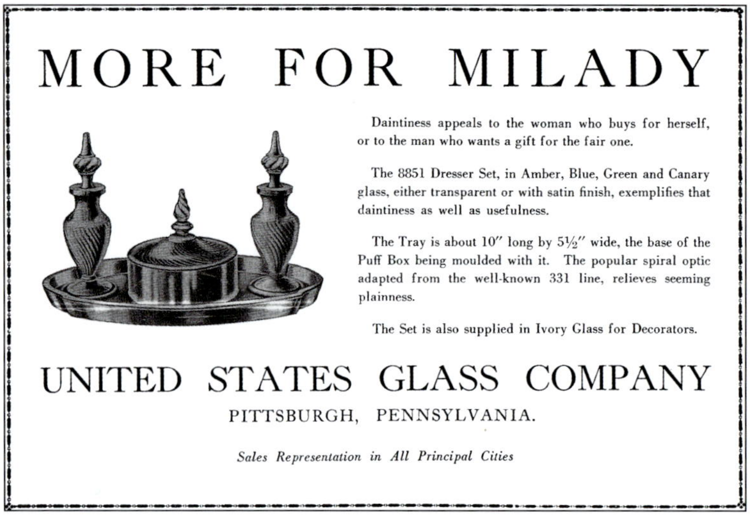

China, Glass and Lamps, 1925, advertisement for the **Milady** Dresser Set.

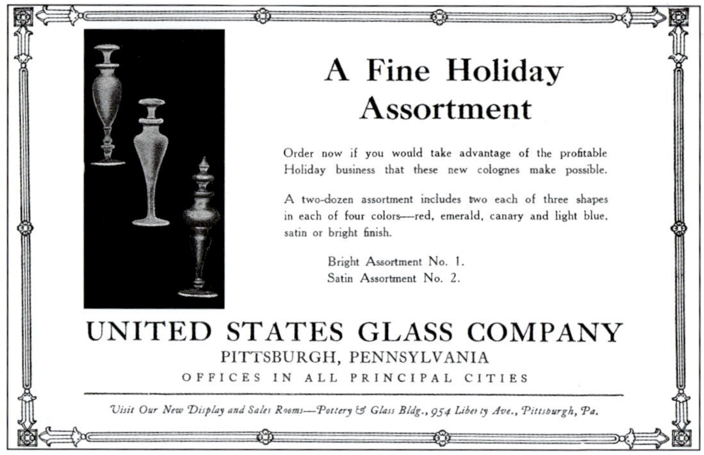

China, Glass and Lamps, October 20, 1924, advertisement showing three new styles of colognes produced at Factory K.

Green (Emerald) #5768, 7.5" h. Cologne, $125.
Green (Reflex) Satin #5772, 4.5" h. Cologne, **No. 14 Parrot** decoration. $65.
Blue Satin, unidentified line number, 4.5" h. Cologne, **Lily of the Valley** cutting. $55.
Ivory #331, 5.5" h. Cologne. $85.
Red #5768, 7.5" h. Cologne. $175.
Red #5770, 5.25" h. Cologne, minus stopper. $85.

China, Glass and Lamps, February 9, 1925, advertisement illustrating three styles of colognes.

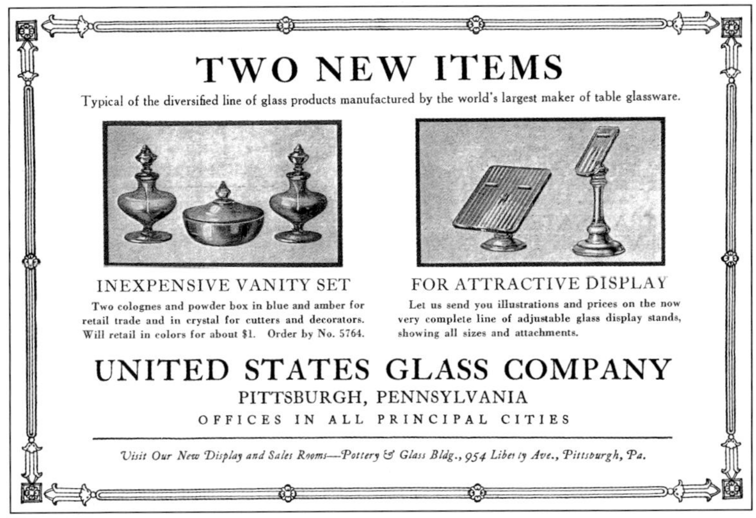

China, Glass and Lamps, September 21, 1925, advertisement which shows the puff box that matches the #5764 colognes.

China, Glass and Lamps, April 28, 1924, advertisement depicts three different cuttings from Factory R.

China, Glass and Lamps advertisement promoting the #5772 dresser set, available in bright or satin finish.

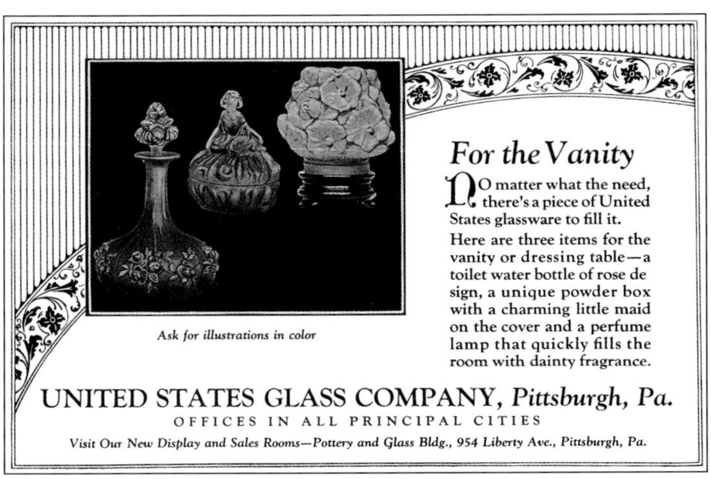

China, Glass and Lamps, February 4, 1924, advertisement showing the #15318 **Rose** Toilet Bottle, #9313 **Dancing Girl** Puff Box, and the **#E-7** Perfume Lamp.

China, Glass and Lamps, May 30, 1922, advertisement picturing the **Milady** Ring Holder. The ring holders are considered scarce.

Pink and Blue, unidentified line number,
10" Dresser Trays, satin finish. $85 each.

THE GLASS OUTLOOK

"Artistic"

The Cutting Superb

A TRANSPARENT band of brilliant golden amber carrying the new "Artistic" cutting illustrated above is the latest contribution from our Glassport designers. It is now offered on the No. 300 Goblet, Sundae, Saucer Champagne, and No. 517 Ice Tea. Only a sample, sent on request, can convey a true idea of its real profit possibilities.

Like Rare Old Glass

Photographic plates and halftones cannot begin to picture the the thousands of blended colors reflected from these two new items,—No. 6858 Tall Colognes with Drip Stopper and and decorated in either Gold or Silver Bronze. These items look like rare old glassware dug from the ruins of Pompeii and are quite different from the ordinary run of colognes.

Dare 'em to Break

Hard work means nothing to these husky members of the United States Glass family. Heavy serviceable tumblers with a thousand uses. The handled tumbler was recently made at the request of a jobber who has found a ready sale for it as a coffee mug. Prices on request.

Have you received a copy of the new price on soda fountain, confectionery and hotel glassware. Sent on request.

UNITED STATES GLASS CO., PITTSBURGH, PA.

7

The Glass Outlook, May 30, 1922.
The #6858 tall colognes are cataloged in Fred Bickenheuser's *Tiffin Glassmasters Book II*. They were available in jasper, royal blue, blue, black, canary, amber, and amethyst, with a bright or satin finish.

Black Satin #15151:
4" Puff Box and Cover. $45.
4" Hair Receiver. $55.

Chapter 11

Ash Trays

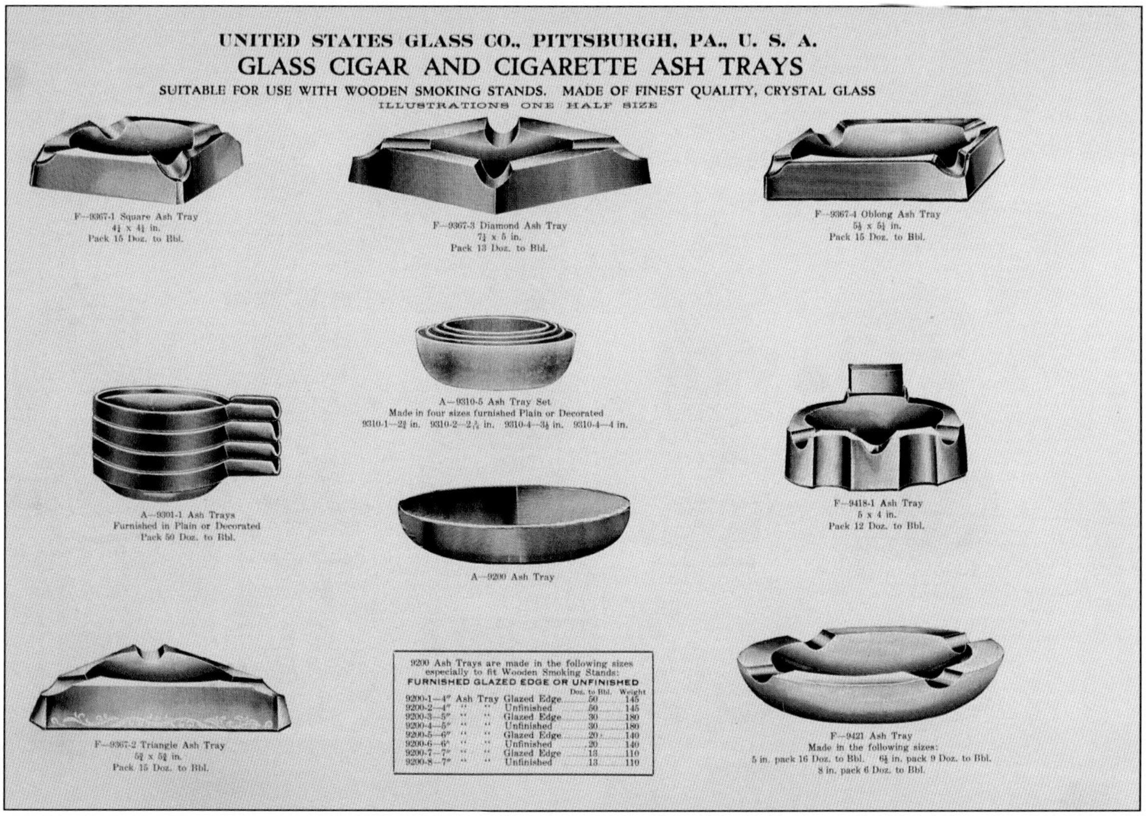

Ash Trays. Undated catalog page, Factories A and F. Top Row: $5, $7, $5. Middle Row: $10 set, $10 set, $4, $5. Bottom Row: $5, $4.

Ash Trays and Smoking Sets. Undated catalog page, Factories A, B, E, G, K, U, and X. Top Row: $10, $8, $65, $10, $10. Upper Middle Row: $10, $10, $15, $10. Lower Middle row: $55, $10, $55, $10, $10. Bottom Row: $8, $8, $55, $8, $8.

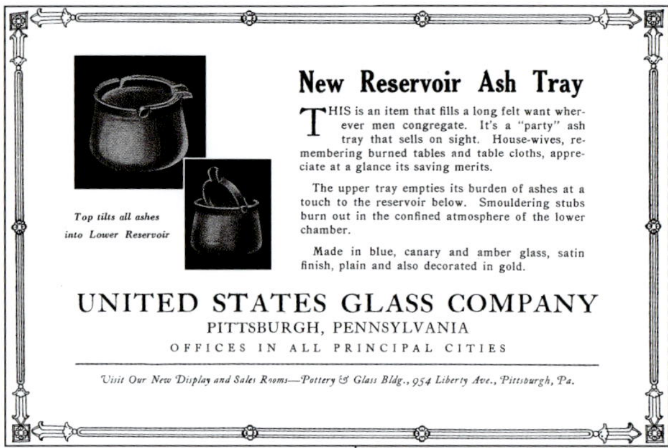

China, Glass and Lamps advertisement, April 21, 1924.

Green Satin #8170 Smoker Set, $115 set. 1.75" ash trays and a 3.75" covered cigarette box fit into recesses in the 6" x 10" pot metal holder. Another style of metal holder was also utilized. Produced in 1928, also known in pink satin.

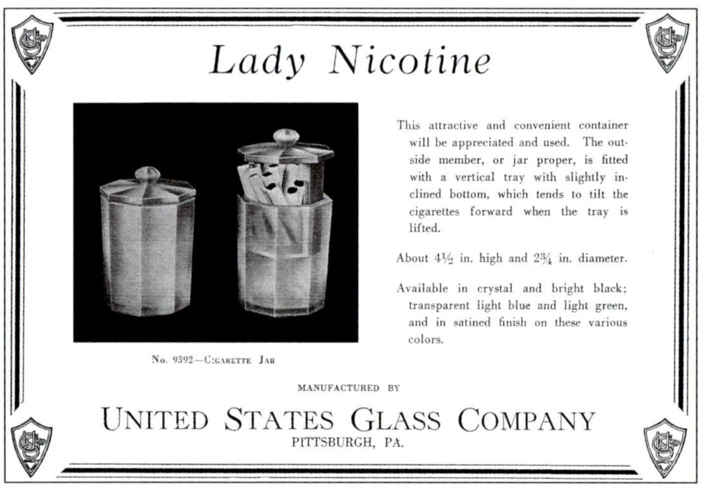

China, Glass and Lamps advertisement, December 6, 1926.

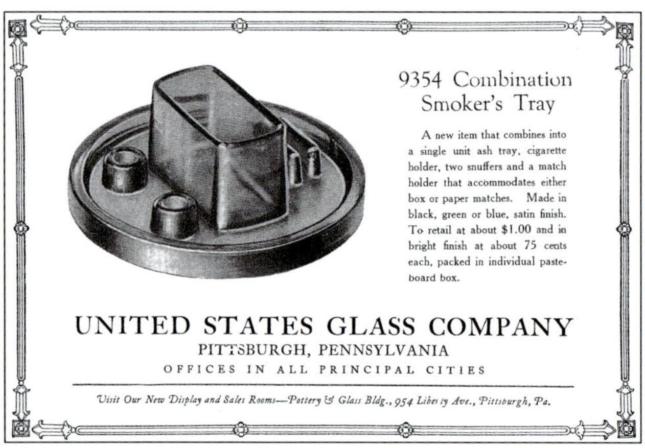

China, Glass and Lamps advertisement, December 7, 1925.

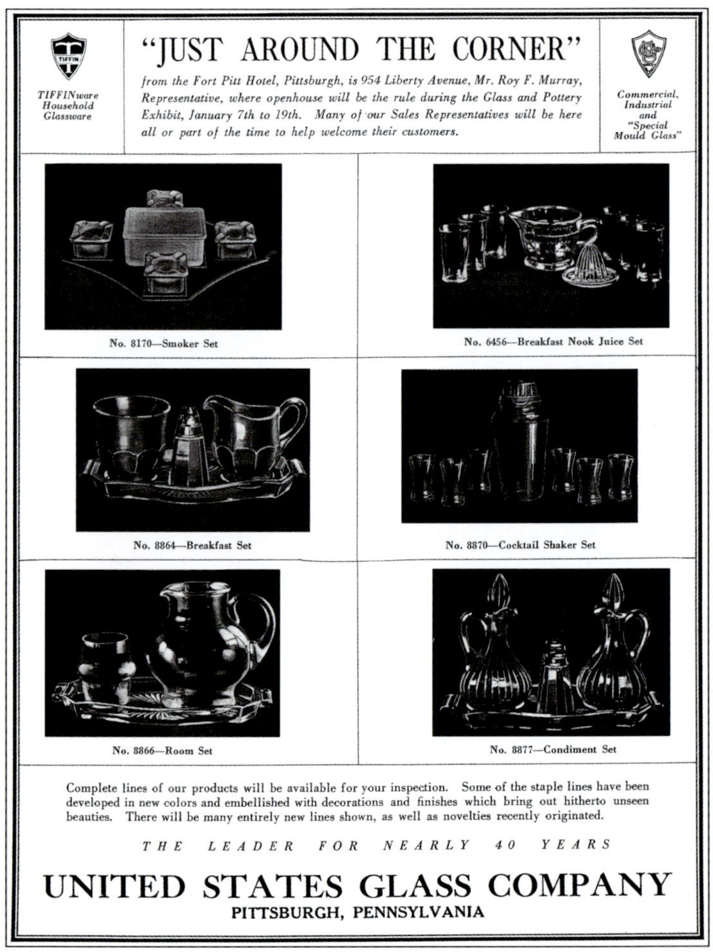

China, Glass and Lamps advertisement, December 24, 1928.

Chapter 12

Undecorated Satin

A satin finish was achieved by immersing the object in an acid bath, comprised primarily of hydrofluoric acid. This treatment created an opaque appearance similar to the texture of satin fabric.

Black Satin. 1927 catalog page, Factory K. Top row: $30, $45 set. Middle Row: $45 set, $35, $75, $35, $65 set. Bottom Row: $55 set, $35, $55, $55 set.

Black Satin. 1927 catalog page, Factory K. Top Row: $55, $125, $65, $55. Middle Row: $30, $30, $55 set, $35, $45 set. Bottom Row: $65, $75 set, $30.

Miscellaneous Colored Ware. Undated catalog page, Factory K.
Top Row: $30, $45, $65 pair, $55 set.
Middle Row: $30, $65 pair, $55, $10.
Bottom Row: $30, $25, $65 pair, $55 set, $55, $125.

Green Satin. Undated catalog page, Factory K.
Top Row: $55 per set.
Middle Row: $20, $35, $35, $20.
Bottom Row: $45, $35, $55, $35, $45.

Finials. Undated catalog page, Factory K. The lamp finials are considered scarce. $35 each.

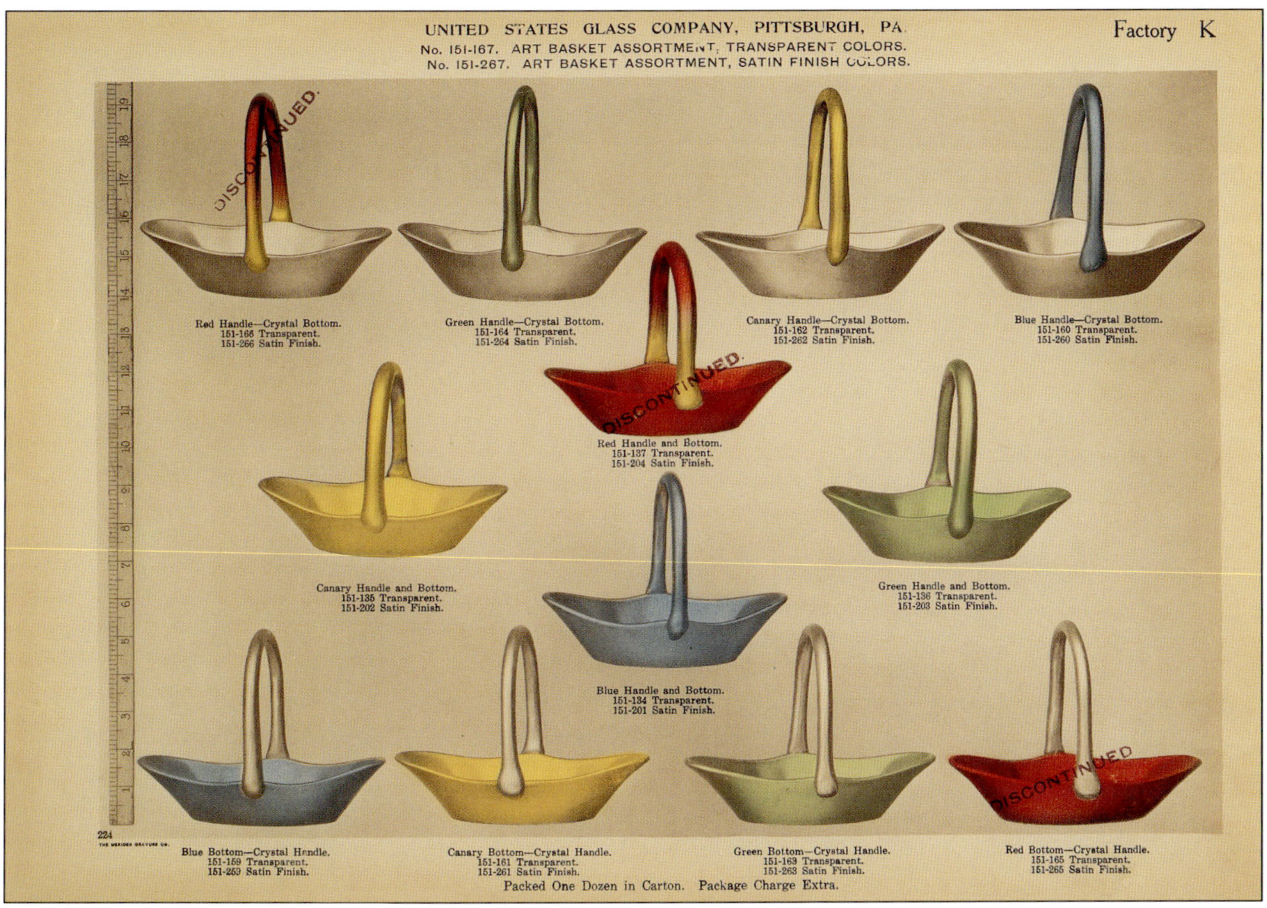

Art Baskets. Undated catalog page, Factory K.
Top Row: $45 each.
Middle Row: $65 each.
Bottom Row: $55 each.

Console Sets. Undated catalog page, Factory B. The #300 number refers to the console set. The line number for the candlestick remains unidentified. Top Row: $95 set. Middle Row: $95 per set. Bottom Row: $75 set.

Console Sets. 1926 catalog page, Factory G. The candlesticks are #79 and the console bowl #320.
Top Row: $85 per set.
Bottom Row: $65 set, $95 set.

Console Sets. 1926 catalog page, Factory G. The candlesticks are #76 and the console bowl #8105.
Top Row: $95 set.
Middle Row: $125 per set.
Bottom Row: $85 set.

Miscellaneous Colored Ware. Undated catalog page, Factory K.
Top Row: $55, $55, $55, $45.
Middle Row: $35 set, $75 pair, $55 set, $35.
Bottom Row: $45 set, $55 set, $35, $55 set.

UNITED STATES GLASS CO. Factory "K" PITTSBURGH, PA. K
MISCELLANEOUS COLORED WARE.

(†) 15179. 9 in. Low Foot Comport, Flared
(‡) 4721. High Foot Grape Fruit, Flared
(*) 15179. Small Sweet Pea Vase and Base
(‡) 15315. 7⅜ in. Low Foot Comport

(*) 15151. 6½ in. Flower Bowl
15151. 8⅜ in. Plate, S. E.
(*) 15151. 9 in. Candlestick
(‡) 15315. 12 in. Low Foot Comport
(*) 15151. 9 in. Candlestick
(‡) 15151. Cheese and Cracker Set

(‡) 15179. 5½ in. Vase, S. E.
(†) 63. 7½ in. Candlestick
(‡) 15151. 9½ in. Berry and Base
(†) 63. 7½ in. Candlestick
(‡) 8308. 6 in. Low Foot Bon Bon and Cover

202

THE MERIDEN GRAVURE CO.

LEGEND

(†) Bright Red, Bright Green, Blue, Canary, Green, Red and Black Satin
(‡) Bright Red, Bright Green, Blue, Canary, Green and Red Satin.
(*) Bright Red, Bright Green, Bright Black, Blue, Canary, Green, Red and Black Satin.

Miscellaneous Colored Ware. Undated catalog page, Factory K. Top Row: $40, $45, $65 set, $45. Middle Row: $40 set, $75 pair, $65, $40 set. Bottom Row: $35, $65 pair, $65 set, $45.

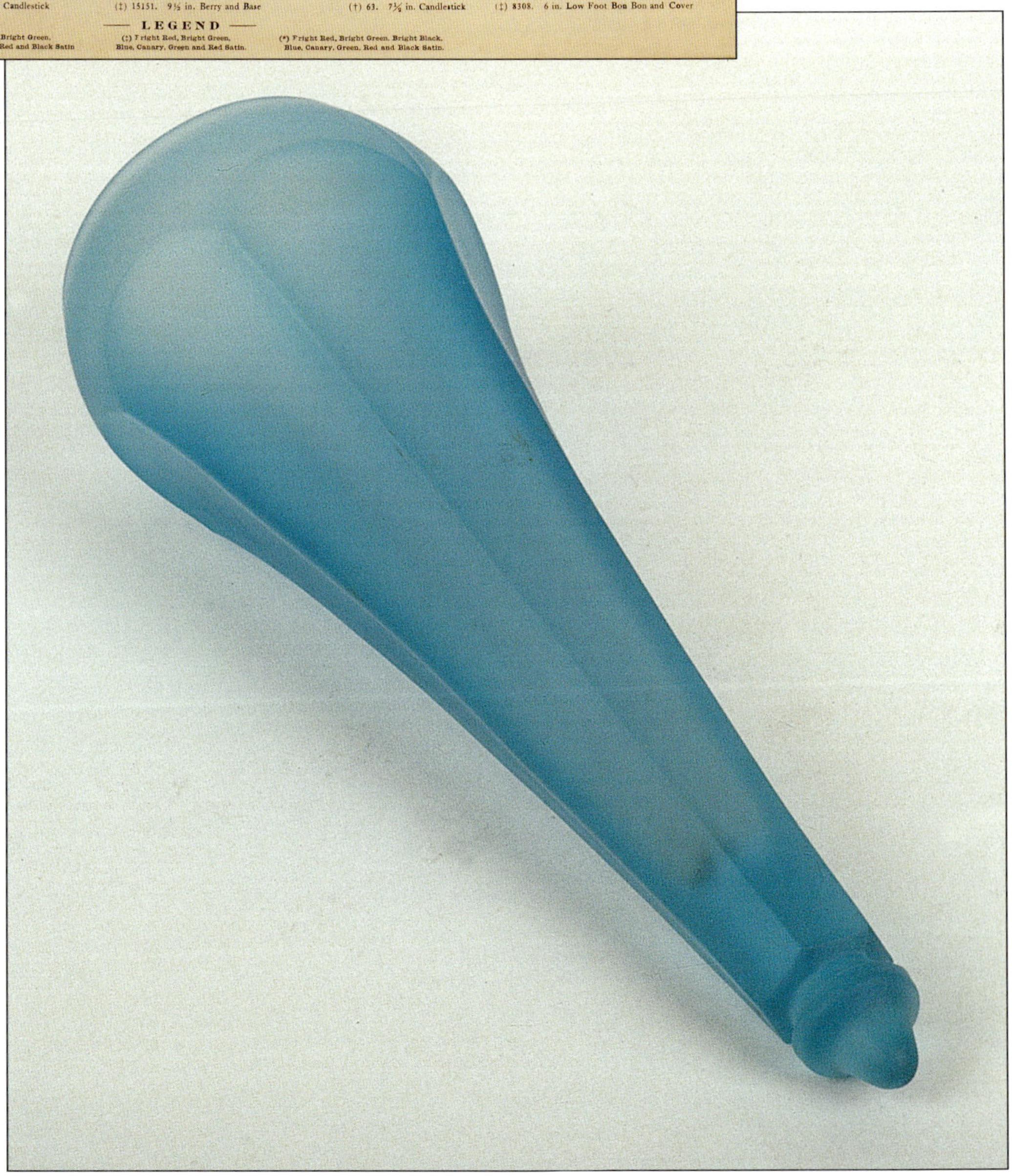

Blue Satin #16259, 8.5" h. Spike Auto Vase. $85. The vase came supplied with a nickel-plated holder and screws.

Canary and Blue #16212, 8" h. Automobile Vases, satin finish, c. 1926. $95, $85. This style of automobile vase is more difficult to find than the #16259 spike automobile vase.

Artistic Table Protectors of Glass

A new item designed to add a touch of color to the dining table and to take the place of the old unsightly fabric pads used under tea and coffee pots and hot dishes. Made in 5, 6 and 7-inch sizes in regular or satin finish—blue, crystal, black or canary color. Satin finished protectors have gold pencil lines as illustrated.

UNITED STATES GLASS COMPANY

General Offices and Salesrooms
South Ninth and Bingham Sts. Pittsburg Pa.

New York: 1107 Broadway, E. T. W. Craig, Representative
Boston: 99 Bedford Street, M. A. Lovell, Representative
Baltimore: 110 Hopkins Place, John A. Dobson Co., Representative
Philadelphia: 10th and Market Sts. J. A. Hemple, Representative
Los Angeles: 643 South Olive Street, J. F. Stirk, Representative
Chicago: 30 East Randolph Street, F. T. Renshaw, Representative
San Francisco: 682 Mission Street, F. M. Dunn, Representative
Dallas: Southland Hotel Building, D. D. Otstott, Inc., Representative
Denver. 404 Jacobson Building, Norton C. Boyer, Representative
St. Louis: 1017 Olive St., J. Donald Fisher, Representative.

China, Glass and Lamps advertisement, July 16, 1923. These low-sitting bases are seldom seen. Also known in green satin.

Black Satin:
Top Row: #9320, 5.75" Base fits a 3.5" bowl. $25.
Bottom Row: #9442, 3.5" Base fits a 2.5" bowl. $20.
#9441, 5" Base fits a 3.5" bowl. $25.
#9440, 6" Base fits a 4.5" bowl. $35.
These are the two most commonly used bases by U. S. Glass. The #9320 base is flat on the bottom and can be found in other sizes. Also available in white satin. The three-footed style base was produced in other colors, including canary, blue, red, jasper, and green. Coral and pearl blues were also utilized on the bases. In advertisements, black colored bases were often used in combination with different colored bowls. Bases were also available in bright finishes.

Green, Blue, and Canary #310, 3.5" h. Favor Baskets, satin finish. $35, $35, $45. Crystal #310, 3.5" h. Favor Baskets, fired-on green, orange, and purple paint. $25 each. The favor baskets were also produced in black, green, pink, and red. Some reproductions have been found, most often in a bright finish.

China, Glass and Lamps advertisement, June 15, 1925.

Amber Satin #78, 11.25" h. Sconce. $215. Considered rare, the sconces were also produced in jasper, canary, royal blue, black, blue, and amethyst with satin finishes, c. 1924.

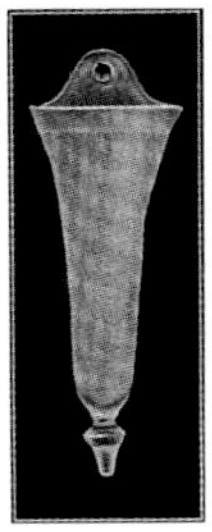

Wall Ornaments of Distinction

These two items—wall vase and wall sconce are among the leaders as wall decorations.

Beautiful in line, and they add a touch of brilliant color in hall, sun parlor, living room or porch.

Satin colors only—black, blue, amber, amethyst, jasper and canary.

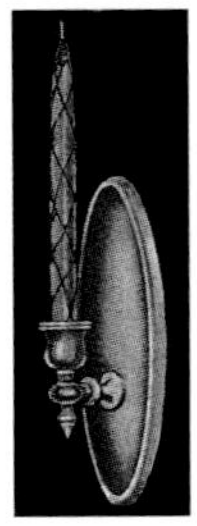

UNITED STATES GLASS COMPANY
PITTSBURGH, PENNSYLVANIA
OFFICES IN ALL PRINCIPAL CITIES

Visit Our New Display and Sales Rooms—Pottery & Glass Bldg., 954 Liberty Ave., Pittsburgh, Pa.

China, Glass and Lamps advertisement, June 23, 1923.

THE GLASS OUTLOOK

A Little Touch of Old Colonial Wall Sconces and Vases

HERE they are—wall sconces and vases that strike a new note in interior decoration. Over the buffet in the dining room, on either side of the breakfast nook, over the fire-place in the living room, at the side of French doors, in the hall, beside the dresser in the bedroom, and in the sun parlor—there's a place for these artistic creations in almost every room. As easy to hang as a small picture,—just drive a nail. Graceful in line and finished in the popular satin colors,—black, blue, canary, amethyst and dark green.

Wall Vase

UNITED STATES GLASS CO., PITTSBURGH, PA.

4

The Glass Outlook, March 1924.

The Glass Outlook

PUBLISHED MONTHLY FOR THE TRADE BY
UNITED STATES GLASS COMPANY, PITTSBURGH, PA.
AND DISTRIBUTED WITHOUT CHARGE

VOL. 1 MAY, 1924 No. 5

Time to Dress Up the Sun Room

THE sun parlor, sun room, or solarium, call it what you will, owes its charm to its lack of formality, its atmosphere of restfulness and its color—color of furniture, floor coverings and hangings.

Colored glassware also adds a touch of harmonious color to tables, walls and windows. We illustrate below three decorative pieces that can be used in several ways. The wall sconce can be used alone between two windows or in the center of a small wall. Two sconces, one on each side of a long window, gives an attractive finish. The same applies to the wall vases; or two sconces and a wall vase in the center make an ideal combination. These items are supplied in satin finish only, in black, blue, amber, amethyst, jasper and canary colors.

The Reflex Green Flower Vase illustrated on the cover is a real gem. The glass carries the faintest tinges of emerald, while the facets of the narrow optics sparkle and scintillate like a diamond in the sunlight. And the design,—have you ever seen a more graceful, artistic modelling in glass?

A larger optic vase and fish bowl, also in Reflex Green, are illustrated on page six.

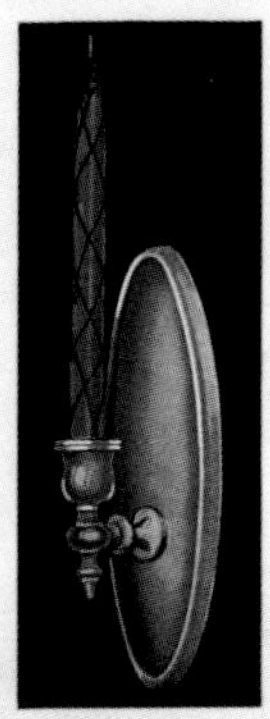

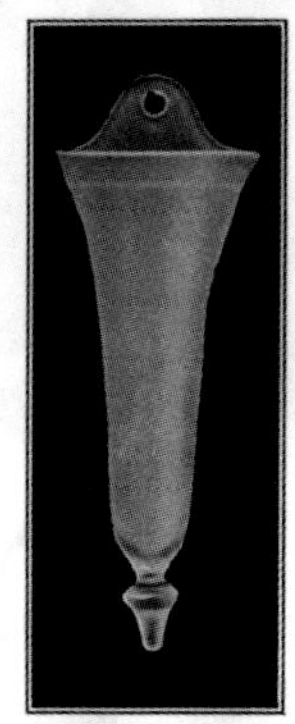

3

The Glass Outlook, May 1924.

Royal Blue Satin #320, 10" h. x 10" w. Wall Console Vase. $275.
Produced at Factory G in the additional colors of black, blue, amber, amethyst, jasper, and canary, with either a bright or satin finish. Occasionally found with a metal holder.

Pink Satin #8308, 5" h. Low Foot Bon Bon and Cover. $45.
Red Satin #8308, 6" h. Low Foot Bon Bon and Cover. $45.
Green Satin #8308, 5" h. Low Foot Bon Bon and Cover. $45.
Note the two sizes of bon bons. The green lid has a block letter "B" on the underside. The 5" size has been found in other colors with a block letter "B" or block letter "C." U. S. Glass may have produced these as private mold work for an outside firm.

Amber Satin, unidentified line number, 8" Open Work Plate. $30.

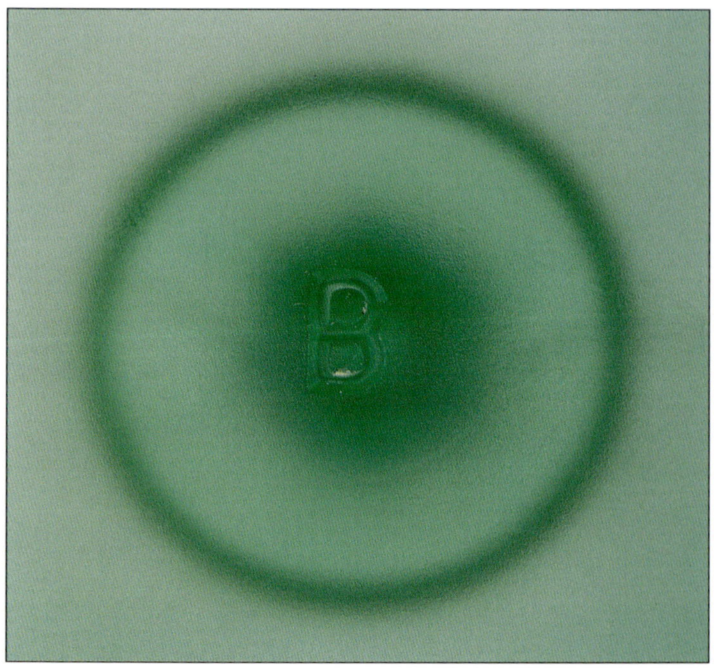

Detail of the embossed block letter "B."

China, Glass and Lamps advertisement, c. 1925.

China, Glass and Lamps, January 28, 1923, advertisement showing the #179 Candy Jar, the #8307 Bon Bon and the #151 Small Lily Vase.

China, Glass and Lamps advertisement, October 5, 1925.

Black Satin #15179, 10" h. Two Handled Candlesticks. $150 pair.
Amethyst #15179, 10" h. Two Handled Candlesticks. $145 pair.
The #15179 candlesticks were also produced in crystal, royal blue, and jasper.

China, Glass and Lamps advertisement, November 3, 1927.

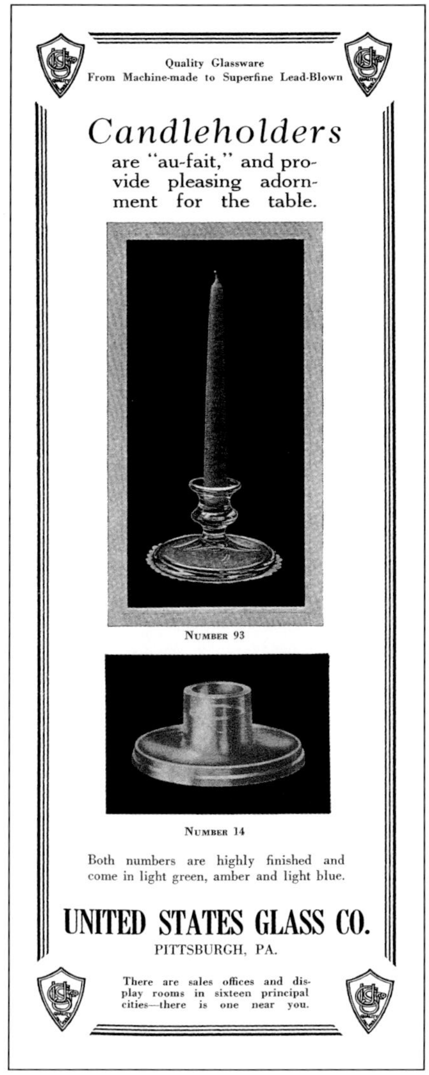

China, Glass and Lamps advertisement.

China, Glass and Lamps advertisement, January 19, 1925.

China, Glass and Lamps advertisement.

China, Glass and Lamps advertisement, November 22, 1926.

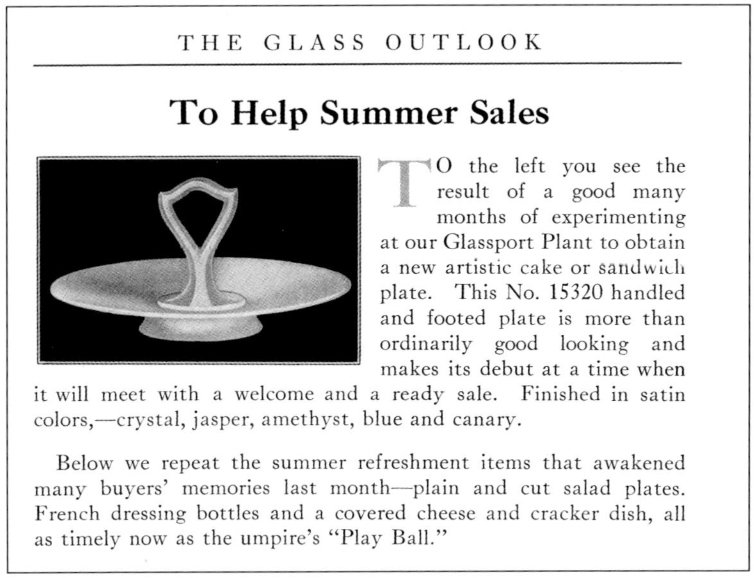

THE GLASS OUTLOOK

To Help Summer Sales

TO the left you see the result of a good many months of experimenting at our Glassport Plant to obtain a new artistic cake or sandwich plate. This No. 15320 handled and footed plate is more than ordinarily good looking and makes its debut at a time when it will meet with a welcome and a ready sale. Finished in satin colors,—crystal, jasper, amethyst, blue and canary.

Below we repeat the summer refreshment items that awakened many buyers' memories last month—plain and cut salad plates. French dressing bottles and a covered cheese and cracker dish, all as timely now as the umpire's "Play Ball."

The Glass Outlook, May 1924, showing the #15320 Handled and Footed Cake Plate.

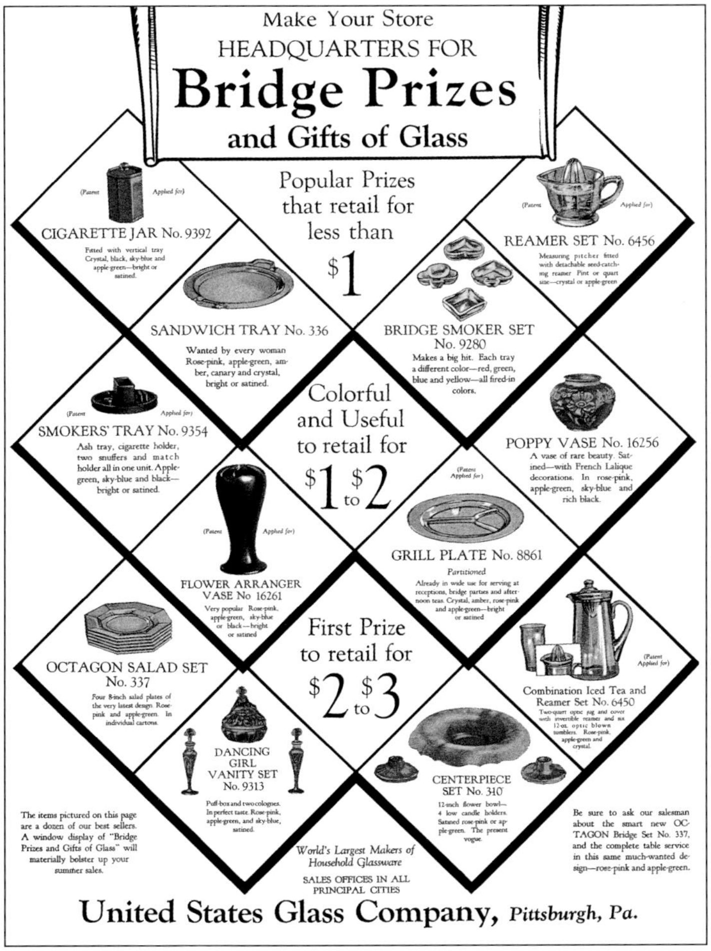

China, Glass and Lamps, c. 1927, advertisement showing various products of U. S. Glass.

China, Glass and Lamps, July 5, 1926, advertisement listing colors and popular items.

Lilac Satin:
#9781, 10" h. Bud Vase. $55.
#9786, 6" h. Rose Bowl. $65.
Produced at Factory R. Lilac is a pale amethyst color and was more commonly used as a trim color on stemware.

Blue #15319, 10" h. Candlesticks. $85 pair.
The upper and lower "balls" of the candlestick have a bright finish, to contrast against the satin finish.

Chapter 13

Miscellaneous

Royal Blue:
#66, 8" h. Candlesticks. $95 pair.
#15319, 10" h. Two Handled Vase. $115.
#15179, 10" Urn Vase. $95.

Canary Satin #151, 6.25" w. x 3.5" h. Vase with Rolled Rim. $65. **Rose.** Blue Satin #15318, 8" Trinket Tray. $75. Canary #151, 5.25" h. Two Handled Vase. $65. The same style vase was also produced in a 10" size. All three items are examples of U. S. Glass opalescent work.

#151, 8" h. Cupped Dahlia Vase. $75.
#84, 10" h. Candlesticks. $95 pair.
#66, 7.5" h. Candlesticks. $95 pair.
The "caramel" color is rare.

#84, 10" h. Candlestick. $45.
#10, 3.75" Low Candleholder. $25.
#15151, 6" h. Cupped Dahlia Vase. $55.
Very few items are found in the "custard" color.

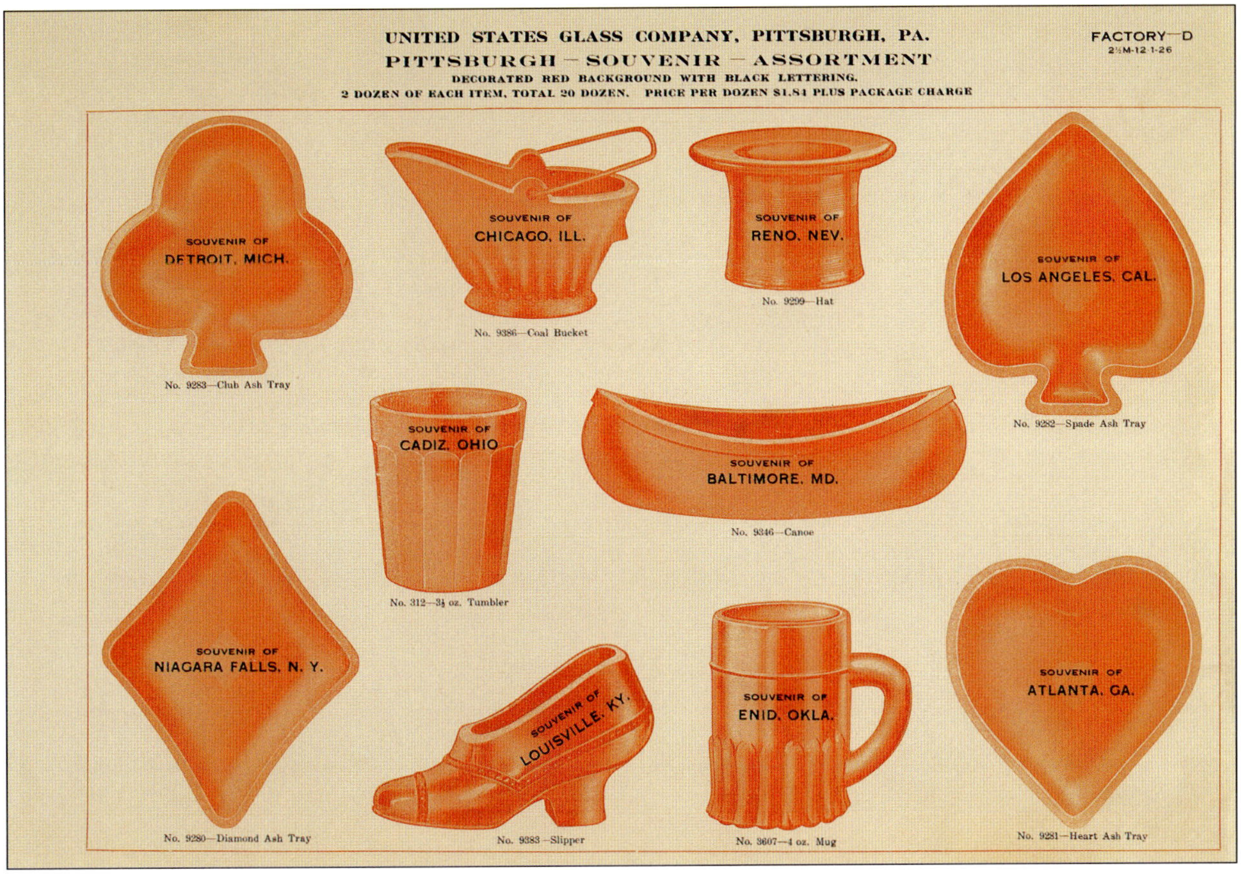

UNITED STATES GLASS COMPANY, PITTSBURGH, PA.

FACTORY—D

2½M-12-1-26

PITTSBURGH — SOUVENIR — ASSORTMENT

DECORATED RED BACKGROUND WITH BLACK LETTERING.

2 DOZEN OF EACH ITEM, TOTAL 20 DOZEN. PRICE PER DOZEN $1.84 PLUS PACKAGE CHARGE

SOUVENIR OF DETROIT, MICH.

No. 9283—Club Ash Tray

SOUVENIR OF CHICAGO, ILL.

No. 9386—Coal Bucket

SOUVENIR OF RENO, NEV.

No. 9299—Hat

SOUVENIR OF LOS ANGELES, CAL.

No. 9282—Spade Ash Tray

SOUVENIR OF CADIZ, OHIO

No. 312—3½ oz. Tumbler

SOUVENIR OF BALTIMORE, MD.

No. 9346—Canoe

SOUVENIR OF NIAGARA FALLS, N. Y.

No. 9280—Diamond Ash Tray

SOUVENIR OF LOUISVILLE, KY.

No. 9383—Slipper

SOUVENIR OF ENID, OKLA.

No. 3607—4 oz. Mug

SOUVENIR OF ATLANTA, GA.

No. 9281—Heart Ash Tray

Souvenirs. 1926 catalog page, Factory D. $15 each.

THE GLASS OUTLOOK

Souvenirs

ARE there any delegations coming to your thriving town or city during 1924? Firemen's Conventions, Chamber of Commerce tours, Rotary, Kiwanis, or other business organization? Go to your local Chamber of Commerce Secretary and find out, because if there are, you want the delegates to carry away a fitting souvenir. Moreover, if souvenirs are to be purchased, you want to sell them.

Ten inexpensive items comprise the well known Pittsburgh Assortment illustrated at right.

For souvenirs or gifts we also suggest the card suit ash trays and the nested cigar rest ash trays below, finished in red, green, blue and yellow.

Also for the smoker we have the tiny cuspidor ash tray in the circle, an exact counterpart of its larger floor-saving brother, which we can also furnish for when the party gets rough.

UNITED STATES GLASS CO., PITTSBURGH, PA.

11

The Glass Outlook, April, 1924, illustrating many souvenir items available from U. S. Glass.

Jade Green #315, 7.5" Low Foot Comport. $65.
There are inventory references to a jade green color produced in the early 1930s. Jadeite is the term glass collectors call this color today.

Chapter 14

Lamps

Novelty Lamps. c. 1924 catalog page, Factory D. Top Row: $375, $395. Bottom Row: $425, $115. The Crinoline Girl Lamp was also marketed as Girl Lamp and Colonial Dame Lamp. The novelty lamps are crystal blanks with painted decorations, atop a bright black base. The Owl and Crinoline Girl Lamp tops had limited production in opal (milk glass).

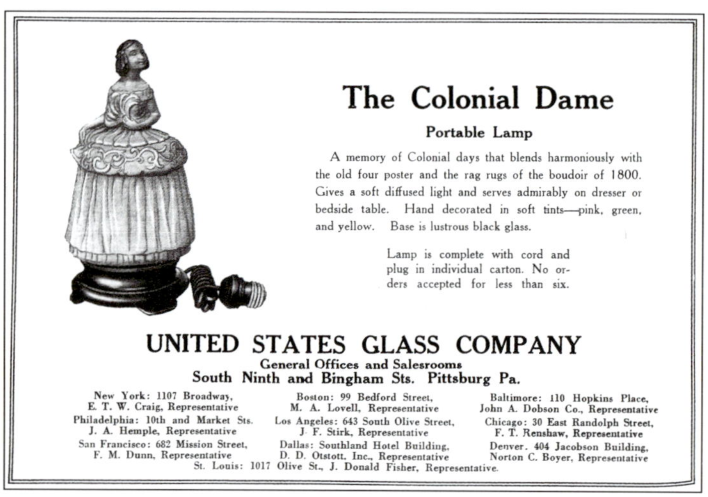

China, Glass and Lamps, May, 1923, advertisement for the Colonial Dame Lamp. Also marketed as the Crinoline Girl lamp.

China, Glass and Lamps advertisement, May 14, 1923.

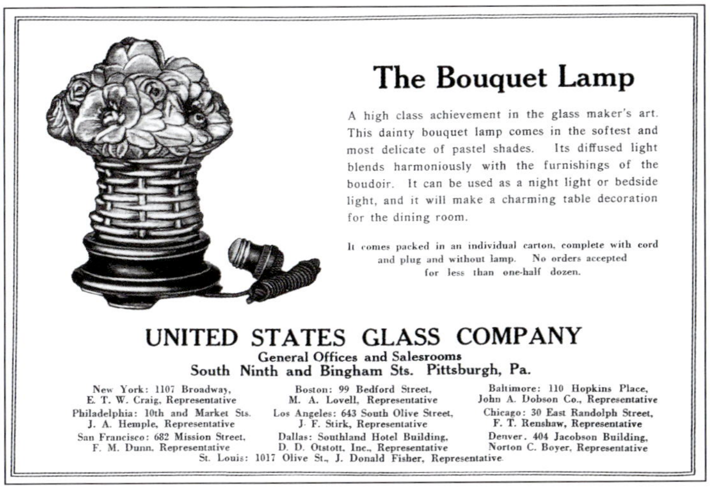

China, Glass and Lamps advertisement, May, 1923. The Bouquet Lamp was also known as the Flower Basket Lamp.

China, Glass and Lamps advertisement, February 18, 1924.

Novelty Lamps. c. 1924 catalog page, Factory D. Top Row: $125, $475, $395, $125. Bottom Row: $425, $325, $425. These novelty lamps are crystal blanks with hand-painted decorations. The Fruit Console Bowl Lamp was produced in several other color combinations. It was also offered with an opal top and base. The Parrot Lamp can be found with red, orange, blue, or green decoration.

Novelty Lamps. 1927 catalog page, Factory D.
Top Row: $395, $425, $395.
Middle Row: $450, $425.
Bottom Row: $1400, $375, $375.

Novelty Lamps. c. 1924 catalog page, Factory D.
$325, $425, $325.
The novelty lamps were manufactured at Factory G, and decorated at Factory D. Several of the lamps were available through 1935.

Boudoir and Novelty Lamps. 1926 catalog page. Top Row: $425, $375, $325, $225, $225, $195, $425. Middle Row: $115, $150, $395, $475, $395, $115, $300. Bottom Row: $325, $375, $375, $1600, $1400, $425, $1000. A July 1930 inventory, Factory D, includes a listing for an Eagle lamp produced on a crystal blank. Along with the Elk lamp, these would have been used by the two fraternal organizations.

China, Glass and Lamps advertisement, October 4, 1929.

#E-13, 14" h. Parrot Lamp. $1000. The #E-13 Parrot Lamp is rarer than the commonly seen #E-6 Parrot Lamp. The #E-13 lamp has a broader base than the #E-6 lamp.

China, Glass and Lamps advertisement, February 14, 1927.

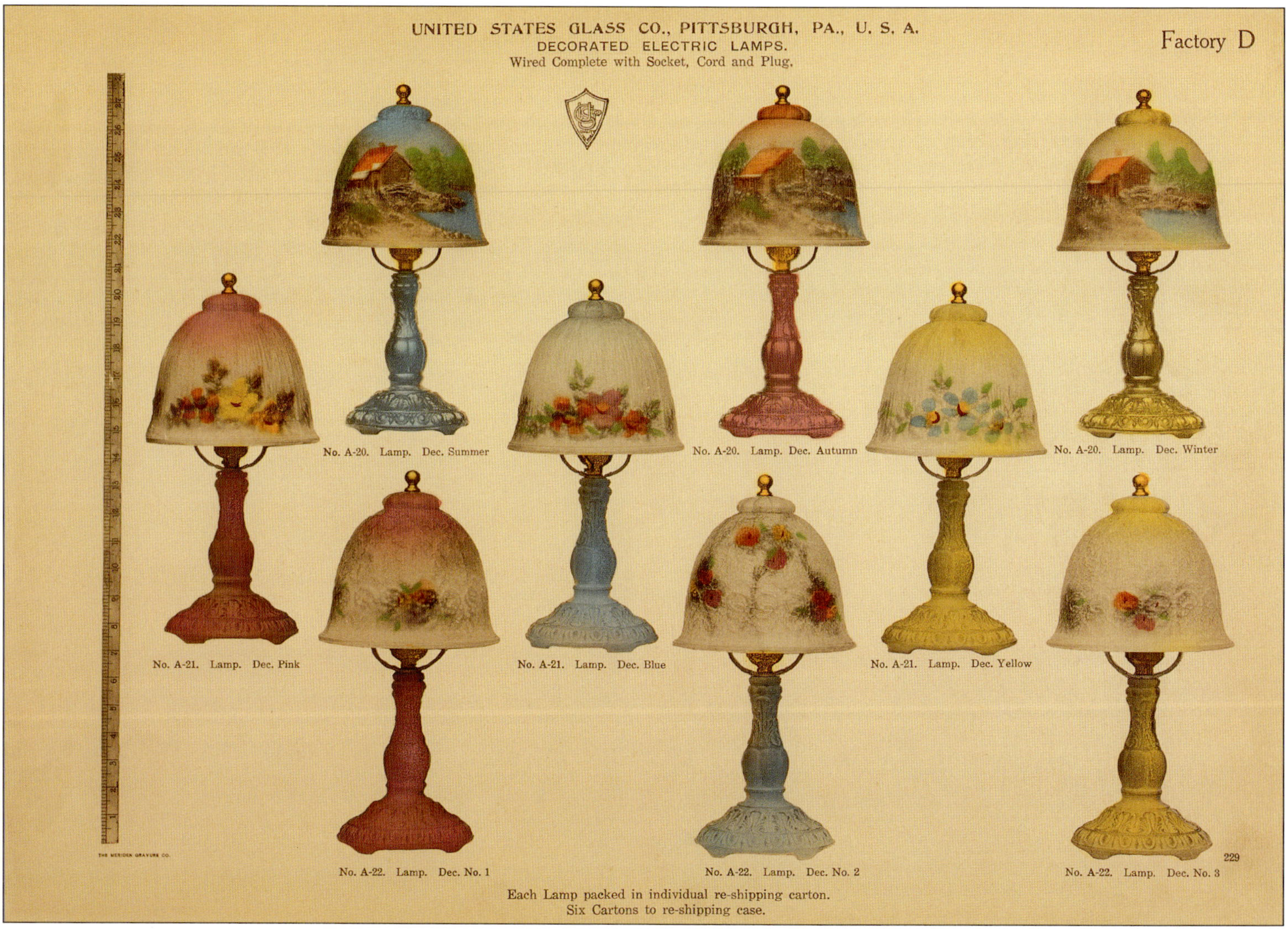

Decorated Lamps. c. 1924 catalog page, Factory D.
Top Row: $325 each.
Middle Row: $225 each.
Bottom Row: $225 each.

Torchiere Lamps. c. 1924 catalog page, Factory D.
Top Row: $115, $125, $125.
Bottom Row: $150 each.

Torchiere Lamps. c. 1924 catalog page, Factory D.
Top Row: $150 each.
Bottom Row: $150, $150, $150, $115, $125, $125.

China, Glass and Lamps advertisement, June 29, 1925.

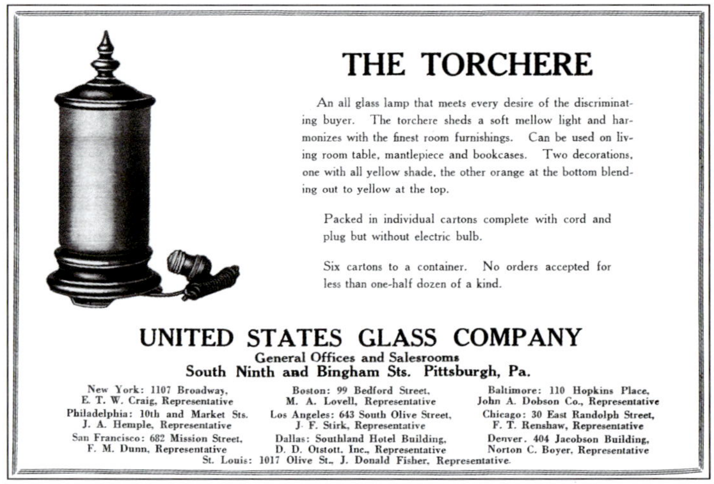

China, Glass and Lamps advertisement, April 23, 1923.

Electric Lamps. c. 1924 catalog page, Factory D. $150 each. Lamps were also marketed as the Bryce portable lamps.

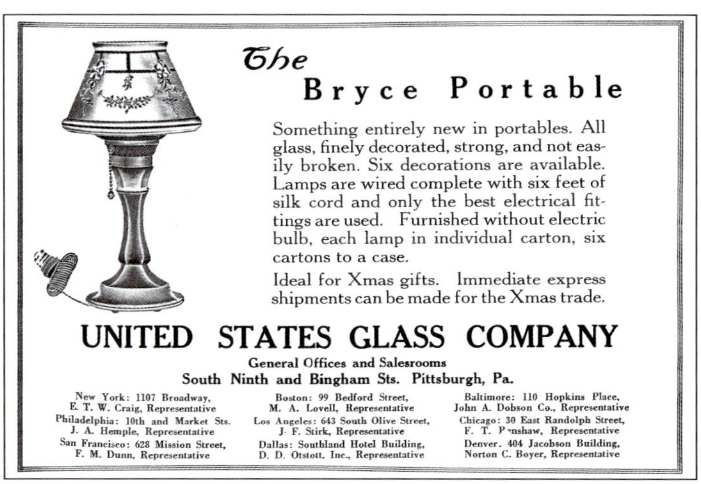

China, Glass and Lamps advertisement, November 20, 1922.

Electric Lamps. c. 1924 catalog page, Factory D.
Top Row: $300 each.
Bottom Row: $300 each.

Electric Lamps. c. 1924 catalog page, Factory D.
Top Row: $300 each.
Bottom Row: $300 each.

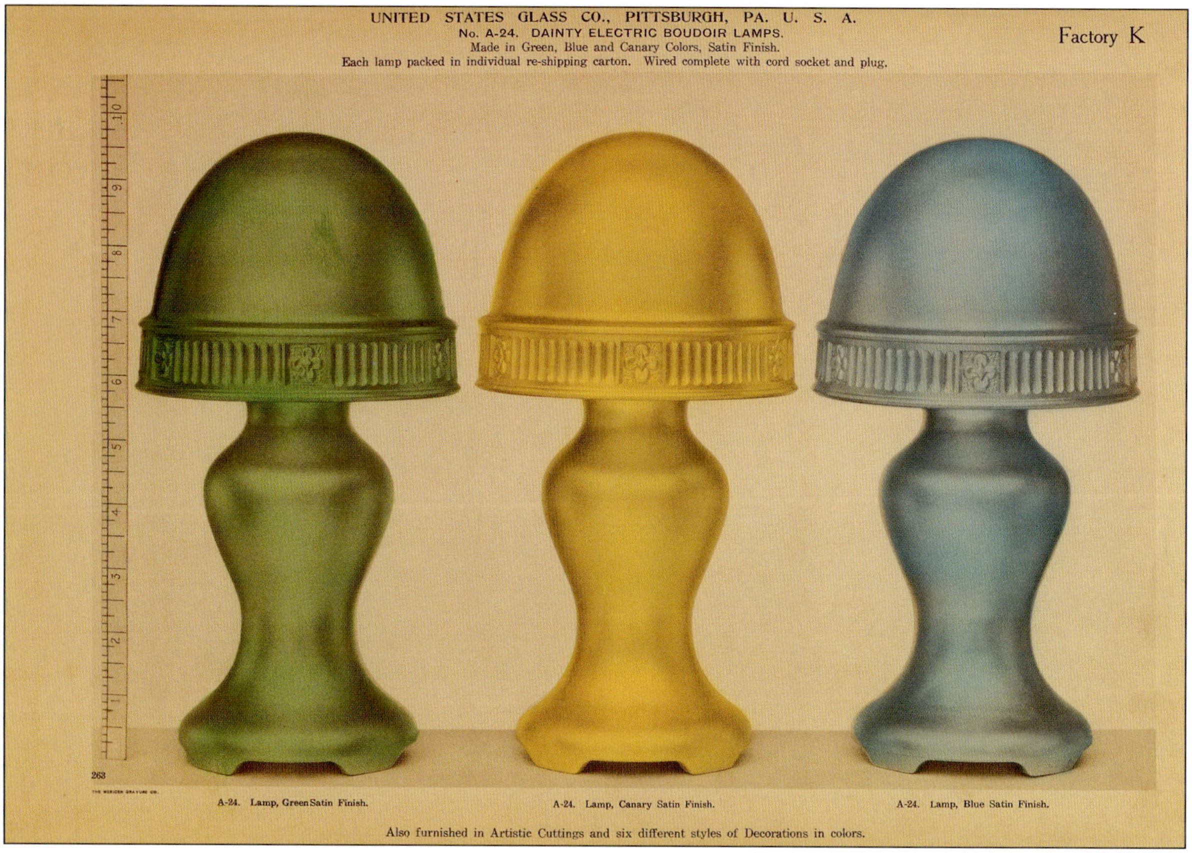

Boudoir Lamps. c. 1924 catalog page, Factory K. $300 each.

Boudoir Lamps. c. 1926 catalog page. The lamps were produced at Factory K, and decorated at Factory D. Note the line number change from #A-24 to #7500.
Top Row: $225 each.
Middle Row: $225, $225, $300.
Bottom Row: $325 each.

China, Glass and Lamps advertisement, November 11, 1926.

China, Glass and Lamps advertisement, November 16, 1925.

Table Lamps. 1927 catalog page, Factory D. $625 each.

Table Lamps. c. 1927 catalog page, Factory D. $625 each.

Torchiere Lamps. 1928 catalog page, Factory D. $175 each.

China, Glass and Lamps, June 28, 1926.

Lamps. 1926 catalog page, Factory D.
Top Row: $225, $225, $195, $195, $195, $225.
Bottom Row: $350 each.

Electric Lamps. c. 1924 catalog page, Factory D. $300 each. The shade is made from the center bowl of the #15318 Rose line.

Electric Lamps. c. 1924 catalog page, Factory D. $300 each.

Electric Lamps. c. 1924 catalog page, Factory D. $425 each.

Electric Lamps.
c. 1924 catalog page,
Factory D. $425 each.

Electric Lamps. c. 1924 catalog page, Factory D. $425 each.

Electric Lamps. c. 1924 catalog page, Factory D. $425 each.

Electric Lamps. c. 1924 catalog page, Factory D. $300 each.

China, Glass and Lamps advertisement, October 25, 1926.

China, Glass and Lamps advertisement, March 9, 1925.

Green #017, 10.5" h. Water Lamp. $85.
Amber #017, 6.5" h. Small Boudoir Water Lamp. $65.
Both water lamps have wide optic and were produced at Factory R. Four other styles of water lamps were also produced in green, amber, pink, and crystal.

Bibliography

Bredehoft, Neila and Bredehoft, Tom. *Hobbs, Brockunier and Company Glass.* Paducah, Kentucky: Collector Books, 1997.

Bickenheuser, Fred. *Tiffin Glassmasters, Book II.* Grove City, Ohio: Glassmasters Publication, 1981.

_____. *Tiffin Glassmasters, Book III.* Grove City, Ohio: Glassmasters Publication, 1985.

China, Glass and Lamps; A Weekly Journal for the Buyer. Pittsburgh, Pennsylvania: Barker, Clarke & Company, 1920s issues.

The Glass Outlook. United States Glass Company trade magazine. Pittsburgh, Pennsylvania, 1924 issues.

Gallager, Jerry. "Consolidated by Tiffin." *Tiffin Glassmasters®.* (Summer 1996): pp. 4-5.

Hallcock, Marilyn R. *Central Glass Company – The First Thirty Years: 1863 – 1893.* Atglen, Pennsylvania: Schiffer Publishing Ltd., 2002.

Heacock, William, and Bickenheuser, Fred. *Encyclopedia of Victorian Colored Pattern Glass, Book 5, United States Glass from A to Z.* Marietta, Ohio: Antique Publications, 1978.

Measell, James and Smith, Don C. *Findlay Glass – The Glass Tableware Manufacturers, 1886-1902.* Marietta, Ohio: Antique Publications, Inc., 1986.

Murray, Melvin L. *Fostoria, Ohio Glass II.* Fostoria, Ohio: 1992.

O'Kane, Kelly. *Tiffin Glassmasters – The Modern Years.* St. Paul, Minnesota: 1998.

Paquette, Jack K. *Blowpipes.* Philadelphia, Pennsylvania: Xlibris Corporation, 2002.

Piña, Leslie, and Gallagher, Jerry. *Tiffin Glass 1914 – 1940.* Atglen, Pennsylvania: Schiffer Publishing Ltd., 1996.

Piña, Leslie, et. al. *Purple Glass – 20th Century American and European.* Atglen, Pennsylvania: Schiffer Publishing Ltd., 2002.

The Pittsburgh Stock Exchange, "Security Committee Bulletin." March 20, 1923. [2 - 4].

The Pittsburgh Stock Exchange, "Security Committee Bulletin." February 27, 1924.

United States Glass Company, Pittsburgh, Pennsylvania, "Nineteenth Annual Report." June 30, 1910.

Weatherman, Hazel Marie. *Colored Glassware of the Depression Era 2.* Springfield, Missouri: Weatherman Glassbooks, 1974.

Webster, James L. *Wheeling Decorating Company.* Paducah, Kentucky: Collector Books, 2003.

Whitmyer, Margaret, and Whitmyer, Kenn. *Bedroom and Bathroom Glassware of the Depression Years.* Paducah, Kentucky: Collector Books, 1990.

Ziegler, Roserita. "Researching with Roserita," *The Glass Review,* April 1981, pp. 34-35.

Indices

Pattern Index

Line Number Index